MEMORIES

by

Irmgard Ruppel

New York City

Cover photo: My first day of school, April 1928, walking down the Siegesallee.

Back cover: Christmas 1932, my father and I on the Zugspitze

FOREWORD

I cannot remember, as a child, understanding all the parts of my mother's amazing life growing up in Berlin before and during the war. The various stories had been told to me, not exactly in order. It was probably when I was 10 or 12 years old that I finally became fully aware of the magnitude of her experience. As a child, I was amazed by the stories of her arrest by the Gestapo, her six months in solitary confinement (with Bismarck's *Gedanken und Errinerungen* to read!), and her brave stance against the Hanging Judge, Roland Freisler. Over the years, as I grew older, the stories strung together began to make sense and I was able to grasp the whole, accurate picture of the first 30 years of her life, 1921-1951.

Nevertheless, time and memory are terrible things that

distort reality and as one gets older the facts become fuzzier and less clear. Now it is more difficult to remember the details of these stories. For most of us, that is, except for my mother. There are few people I know who have a clear recollection of what they wore 46 years ago, what they ate 33 years ago, and the first and last name, and maybe even the birth date, of an acquaintance she has not seen for 40 years.

So it is all the more appropriate that my mother undertook a year ago to write her memoirs of the most interesting part of her life – growing up in Berlin. She did not do this to bring attention to her fascinating life experience, but to convey to her descendents, children, grandchildren, eventually her great-grandchildren the story of their mother, grandmother, and great-grandmother. Only my mother knows the details much better than Tom and I and we owe her thanks for recording these memories. I know my children, but also cousins and friends will enjoy this extraordinary autobiography.

My mother's memoirs are a contribution not only to our family but also to what is sure to become a lapse in memory of the Nazi era. As time passes, those who lived then and can remind us of the horror of that time are vanishing. These like my mother are some of the last survivors who can answer the questions we have about those times. *Memories* has great enduring value to our family and to others – historians, scholars, and friends.

These memories are all the more amazing in their detail for

historical events, facts, background, and descriptions of people and dialog. As you will read, someone who finished her formal education at the age of 15 wrote this! By my record, my mother rates a *"Prima Inter Pares."*

We who worked on this project are proud to have been a part of this effort to publish *Memories*. I am indebted to Heide Loefken who provided the impetus to get Mother to write this book and provided invaluable editorial insights during the early stages of the project, and to my brother, Thomas, who spent innumerable hours scanning and typing and proofing early versions of the manuscript. As a publisher, I have been involved in many, many books. *Memories* has been the most gratifying to have worked on and I am so pleased and proud to have been a part of this book.

Philip Ruppel
Riverside, Connecticut

For my sons, Thomas and Philip, and their families.

These remembrances of things past would have never been written without the encouragement and help of my friend Heide Loefken. She thought that I had a story to tell and insisted that I should write it down. And here it is.

Chapter 1

CHILDHOOD

My story begins in Berlin, during the roaring twenties. I was born in our home – a large apartment on the banks of the Spree River – on October 5, 1921. This was three years after the end of World War I.

The country was still reeling from the losses of the "Great War." Germany, of course, had lost the war and was assessed to pay huge reparations to the Allies. As a result, the German Mark devalued and finally became worthless. Millions of people became poor.

My father was a civil servant at the Treasury and my mother at that time went to his office at noon every day to pick up his pay to buy groceries because the next day money would be worth even less.

The defeat of Germany brought not only great financial

but also political turmoil. The new Republic had no democratic foundation. Disgruntled officers formed paramilitary organizations, intending to overthrow the new center- and left-of-center government. They blamed the defeat on a "stab in the back" by Jews and Socialists. Assassinations of politicians became frequent in the early 1920s. The most prominent of those killed was the Foreign Minister Walter Rathenau who was shot to death in an open car on the way to his office from his house in Grunewald in 1922. He was a great patriot, an intellectual, and a Jew and had been a target for right-wingers for years. Just as the shooting broke out, my two cousins, one a baby in a carriage and the other one three years old, were passing by with their nanny. There was a hail of fire but they were not hurt.

My father was born in Hamburg in 1885. He was the oldest of three children, two of whom died before him: his sister Tilly of diphtheria at the age of nine and his brother Edgar. Edgar was my godfather but I never knew him since shortly after my birth he moved to Buenos Aires. On his first home-leave in 1929, at the age of 32, an epidemic of scarlet fever broke out on board ship and he died a week after he landed in Hamburg. Nowadays with antibiotics both diphtheria and scarlet fever are easily cured. His death was a great blow to my father. I have always thought that perhaps, had Edgar lived, the story of my family might have turned out differently as my father might have left Germany and linked up with his brother abroad.

I did not know my grandfather who died before I was born but my father's mother came to live with us in Berlin in the early 1920's after having lost most of her savings in the inflation. I loved her very much, called her Unni, and it was she who really brought me up. My mother adored me but did not want to be bothered with the details of child rearing.

Photos of my grandmother show her as an old lady though she was barely 60 when she came to live with us. Women at that time and at that age wore long skirts, high-buttoned shoes, and high lace collars to conceal wrinkled necks.

I was an only child and did not have any playmates. I had to amuse myself, playing and later reading tons of books. Dolls were boring but I had lots of lead-soldiers that I lined up for parades and battles, keeping me busy for hours. Books became my best friends: "Nesthaekchen," a Nancy Drew-type series, Karl May, all about Indians and cowboys, "Emil and the Detectives" by Erich Kaestner, and when I was a little older, history, which became my favorite subject in school. I went to my father's bookcases and read memoirs and biographies.

My grandmother believed that every girl should learn to knit, crochet, and embroider which did not tempt me in the least when I could read interesting books.

We lived in a large ten-room apartment on the banks of the Spree River until I was eleven when we moved around the corner into an even larger one with twelve rooms. In our first apartment there was no central heating but every room had a coal burning tile-stove which gave off plenty of heat. All the rooms were the size of a New York one-bedroom apartment. During the winter-season, my parents gave dinner-parties for 30 or 40 seated at a long table in the dining room. We had a couple. He was the butler and she cooked but for parties a caterer sent two chefs with white toques to prepare the food. I found parties very exciting except for the fact that I had to say hello and curtsey to the guests before dinner.

My parents went out a great deal, especially during the winter-season, but we always had lunch together, and my father often came home for the hot meal of the day. Conversation frequently touched on politics and, since I had nothing better to do, I listened. For example, I remember when an American delegation came to Berlin, headed by Parker Gilbert of J.P. Morgan, to negotiate the Dawes and Young Plan to help Germany pay for the reparations. Since my father was in the Treasury, he was involved. And early on I heard about the Nazis and Communists, the frequent changes of government, and the financial problems of the Republic. My interest in politics thus started in my childhood.

My parents were great opposites. My father was an intellectual who had been educated at a humanistic "Gymnasium" where the languages taught were Greek and Latin. He had been first in his class, *Primus Inter Pares* (first among equals), and could not understand that not everybody was equally smart. My mother had a sunny disposition and was determined to get the most fun out of life. She had detested school and never set foot in mine. Books did not interest her and I still hear her saying: "I read in the book of life," whatever that was. She was a great optimist whereas my father was rather pessimistic. Unfortunately he was to be proven right. My parents complemented each other and were very compatible.

When I was a little older, ten or eleven, I loved talking to my father about all kinds of subjects -- history, foreign countries etc. -- which made me feel quite grown-up. He was not patient and could not understand why math and algebra were a problem for me. When I was in my teens he tried to teach me bridge, then and now considered a social grace. I could never remember my cards, let alone my partner's; he got very red in the face, declared me a total idiot and threw the cards down. That was the end of that.

My mother came from a large family; there were seven of them, four boys and three girls. My grandfather, Benno Orenstein, was a self-made tycoon who in the Industrial Revolution founded a worldwide enterprise that manufactured locomotives and railroad equipment, Orenstein & Koppel, which exists to this day. He was born in Posen, West Prussia, in 1851. His father died early and it fell to Benno to support his family. His school reports showed him to be an average student. With a loan of 3,000 marks from a wealthy uncle he went to Berlin where in 1876 at the age of 25 he started a business in scrap-metal with a partner Arthur Koppel. Within a year, Benno repaid the loan and opened the first factory near Potsdam making railroad equipment. This plant, Drewitz, would employ 7,500 workers who were given generous social benefits. The partner Koppel was eventually bought out but his name stayed on because by then Orenstein & Koppel was known worldwide.

My grandfather had made a personal fortune of 20 million gold marks at the beginning of the First World War and was one of the richest men in Germany. He signed 8 million in war-bonds, later worthless, and much melted away in the inflation. Yet life remained comfortable.

My grandmother Rosa Landsberger came from a very well to do family who had been in Berlin for more than a hundred years. In 1883, she brought into the marriage a considerable dowry.

As much as Benno was a success in business, at home life was much different. His sons feared him and his wife periodically retreated to sanatoriums to soothe her nerves amongst other rich patients equally afflicted. When World War I broke out, all four sons immediately volunteered for military service. Two of them did not come back.

The three daughters had a much easier time. Being girls they were not under pressure from their father. Their aim in life was to find a suitable husband.

My mother was the oldest. There were two governesses, one for the older and one for the younger children. They lived on Hohenzollernstrasse, off Tiergartenstrasse. Later my grandparents moved to a large house on Lake Wannsee.

I remember Sunday lunches at my grandparents with aunts, uncles, and cousins. At the long table, the children sat together. A lot of the grown-ups' conversation was about money. My father, red in the face, became increasingly impatient listening to these endless discussions. My grandfather died when I was four, days after the celebration of the 50th anniversary of his firm. I remember only one time when I was alone with him. He took me to his greenhouse and presented me with a flowerpot, promptly confiscated by my mother who said it would give me a rash. I had hoped for a toy. The house and garden look exactly today as in my childhood. I had eight cousins but only saw them at birthday parties. We were never close.

The entertainment at my parties was silent films, black and white, with Charlie Chaplin as the tramp and Harold Lloyd dangling from skyscrapers, a success because children were not usually taken to the movies. I was seven when I first went to the theater to see "Little Red Riding Hood" which impressed me so that I remember it to this day.

Our apartment house, built before the turn of the century, was on the Spree River and I loved to see the barge-traffic go by. The owners and their families lived on board. A clothesline typically flapped in the wind, a little barking dog ran back and forth and a pot with red geraniums brightened the decor. Coal, lumber, and many industrial goods were shipped on the river and traffic was lively.

There was a railroad station across the Spree and one day in 1928 I watched a motorcade of two cars crossing the bridge. It was King Amanullah of Afghanistan on a state-visit.

I rode my tricycle and scooter up and down the long hallway in our apartment. The only telephone was on the wall with a crank. A telephone operator connected you with your party. Everybody knew his or her operators. There were two of them, and at Christmas they got presents from their customers with whom they were on chummy terms.

Back then the school year started in April and I was 6½ when my education began. My mother did not want to send me to a public elementary school where, according to her, I would be with unpleasant children and catch all their illnesses. It was decided to have me tutored privately together with a little boy my age. As it turned out my schoolmate was ill so often that I had the teachers to myself. School was mostly at my house.

Miss Kallmann, my teacher whom I liked very much, taught everything but history and religion. A teacher from the Lycee Francais covered those subjects. With so much individual attention I was able to cover the four-year program in three years after passing a so-called intelligence test. I was then entered in the Sexta (the first grade after primary school) of the Mommsen-Schule, an all-girls school, the equivalent of Chapin or Spence in New York. It was run by Adelheid Mommsen, a daughter of the famous Roman historian Theodor Mommsen.

Our school was located on the ground floor of an old-fashioned apartment house near the Kurfuerstendamm. The rooms were dark and dingy and the facilities altogether quite depressing. For recess we went out to a small courtyard and ate our eleven o'clock sandwiches while in neighboring yards housewives beat the dust out of their carpets on the line. Miss Mommsen carefully selected the student-body, comprised of "Berlin Society." The daughters of the British Ambassador were delivered and picked up in a Rolls Royce.

We were 12 to a class and had two days a week off, (one day in the higher grades), because with small classes and individual attention we still achieved the norms set by the Education Ministry. There was a half-day of school on Saturday.

For the first time in my life I was together with other girls and able to form friendships. I was driven and picked up by our chauffeur but what I really wanted was to take the Elevated – or S-bahn -- from Lehrter Bahnhof together with some girls who lived in the neighborhood. My mother was firmly against it and it took a couple of years until she finally gave in.

Motor-traffic was not a danger in those days. My mother let me go under the condition that our butler would walk me halfway to the station where I would meet a friend. That was very embarrassing and I prevailed upon him to walk several steps behind me. Eventually I got rid of my escort. The girl who lived closest to me was Ursula Cyliax (later von Schlieben). She was not in my class but we became good friends and travelled to and from school together.

On the Moltke-Bridge we met most mornings an army non-com in uniform who worked in the War Ministry nearby and who said hello to us, which made us feel quite grown-up. One morning he, in civilian clothes, turned out to be a flasher. We were horrified but then decided to put an end to this problem. Next time we would see him we would walk arm in arm, I would push Ursel against him and that, we thought, should send a message. This was exactly what happened and we never saw him again. I swore Ursel to secrecy; on no account should she tell her mother who immediately would tell my mother who would condemn me then to eternal chauffeuring. But perhaps my mother had a point; danger can lurk anywhere.

My favorite subjects in school were German, English, history, and geography whereas math and natural sciences did not interest me. Every morning I wondered whether the school had perhaps burned down overnight whereupon I could go home and enjoy myself. And so it was, but only six years after I graduated, the house was destroyed in an air raid.

I had always wished for a dog and eventually I got a wire-haired fox terrier named Marko with an illustrious pedigree, sweet but very stupid. The moment he was off the leash he would run away, never find his way back, and give us a lot of trouble. After I did my homework I would take him for long walks and together we explored the old parts of the inner city, most of which were later destroyed. I thus came to know many of the historical buildings, now gone.

We moved from Kronprinzenufer to Alsenstrasse, around the corner, because my grandmother had severe arthritis and could not climb stairs anymore. In our new apartment we had an elevator that opened up directly inside our entrance hall, which my friends found very interesting. Alsenstrasse was a short street, tree-lined, and very quiet, with several foreign legations on the block.

Our apartment was beautiful and much more modern than the old one with more bathrooms, central heating and a large balcony where we ate our meals in warm weather.

In the fall of 1932, my parents gave a luncheon party for 25. Among the guests was Prince Heinrich, the consort of Queen Wilhelmina of Holland. He was only allowed to travel accompanied by courtiers who acted as minders because he had a roving eye. For me the most memorable moment that day was when Marko, my dog, escaped through an open door and was nowhere to be found until hours later an unemployed person brought him home. Our address was on the dog collar.

I got a small allowance that I spent on movies. There were two small cinemas on Unter den Linden. The first film I saw, which made a lasting impression on me, was Noel Coward's "Cavalcade," the story of an English family, from the siege of Mafeking in the Boer War to the 1930's, similar to "Upstairs, Downstairs."

In my childhood, there was no such thing as "going

shopping." One bought what one needed but clothes were generally made by dressmakers or by a seamstress for me who came to the house twice a year, before summer and winter. Children's clothes were unimaginative and looked the same. I greatly envied a girl in my class who wore a burgundy sweater from Braun, an elegant clothing store in Unter den Linden. It took a full year to convince my mother that I desired such a sweater more than anything else. She thought it ridiculous to buy something from an expensive store that I would wear to school but I finally wore her down. It became my favorite item of clothing and it lasted until both elbows had holes.

When I was ten and eleven I attended dancing-classes, conducted by two proper ladies who had fled the Baltic regions, then occupied by the Bolsheviks, after World War I. They were very keen on good manners and deportment. The classes were held in the apartments of the students. One place we liked best, a palais by the Brandenburg Gate, belonged to the grandmother of a schoolmate. You drove into the entrance where, on the staircase, the major domo in tails announced: "Fraeulein Zarden." The foot-men wore knee breeches and the class was held in the ballroom, a replica of the Hall of Mirrors in Versailles. We learned the Fox Trot, Waltz and Tango and also the Quadrille, all of which gave us ample opportunity to step on each other's toes

During recess we stuffed ourselves at the delicious buffet with cakes and ice cream and looked much the worse for it. The only mother who often came to watch us was Frau von Ribbentrop whose two children were in our class. I can still see her sitting on the sofa with our hostess, Frau von Friedlaender-Fuld. Before the Nazis came to power

Ribbentrop was a salesman for his father-in-law's "Henkell Sekt," the champagne firm. A few years later Frau von Friedlaender-Fuld had to leave Germany because she was Jewish. She died in her 80's during the war in the South of France of malnutrition and neglect, a cruel fate after a life of great luxury. Joachim Ribbentrop, who had become Hitler's Foreign Minister, one of the worst Nazis in power, was sentenced to death at the Nuremberg War Crimes trials and hanged. To this day the Ribbentrop family regards him as a hero.

When I was 12 or 13, my parents decided that I should have riding lessons in a riding-academy near the Tiergarten, Berlin's Central Park, where my mother and her sisters had been riding when they were young. My teacher's father had taught them. Herr Leistner had been a cavalry sergeant in the First World War and was a wonderful Berlin type. One of his favorite sayings was, "Jnaediges Frollein, nu haenge'se mal nich auf'm Jaul wie 'ne Waescheklamme uff 'ner Waescheleine." ("Miss, now don't hang on that horse like a laundry pin on the clothes line.")

I enjoyed this sport very much, except when I was made to jump over hurdles and fell off. After a few years my teacher thought that I should have my own horse instead of a different one every time. My parents agreed. The Tiergarten had many different bridle paths and you would meet lots of riders. From the stables to the park it was only a block but the traffic and the exhaust of the buses would make my horse extremely skittish. I rode for many years, even during the war, until the fall of 1941 when the Army drafted all horses, including mine, for the Russian campaign. I have often wondered how this poor animal fared in battle-noise. Before the war the riding academy was taken over by the Army High Command and it was in this building that the officers who had plotted to assassinate Hitler on July 20, 1944, were arrested, and some of them executed on the spot.

Chapter 2

BERLIN LIFE

Berlin during the Weimar Republic was a vibrant and lively metropolis, socially and especially culturally. Theaters, operas, concerts, museums, art-galleries, and the literary scene flourished. This changed drastically with the Nazis coming to power and the eviction of the Jews from all aspects of public life. Berlin society before 1933 was an unusual mix of leaders of industry, banking, public servants, diplomats, writers, journalists, artists, and academics. Berlin was not only the capital but also the most interesting and diverse city in Germany. I only learned from books after the war that it also had a naughty and seedy side that attracted people from all over the world in search of excitement, drugs, and sex.

Everybody who was famous turned up sooner or later in Berlin. I remember Erich Maria Remarque at a tea party my mother gave. He was very good-looking and in great demand in society. The film about World War I, based on his best-selling book "All Quiet on the Western Front," had just opened to great success but also violent demonstrations by the Nazis in the movie-house because of its pacifist message. Ten years later they got what they wanted, World War II.

I sometimes saw famous people. Governments changed often before Hitler took over. In 1928 I witnessed with my parents on the steps of the Reichstag the swearing-in of a new chancellor, Hermann Mueller.

During the summer we spent some time every year at Heiligendamm, a beautiful resort on the Baltic Sea. One morning in 1931, I came down and found the courtyard of the hotel full of people, men, women, and children who did not look at all like guests. My mother was not up yet. I asked what was going on and was told: "Hitler is on a campaign tour through Mecklenburg with Goering and Goebbels." Of course I had heard of him, his growing power in parliament and the bloody street-fights with Communists.

I did not have to wait long till Adolf came out in his brown shirt with fat Goering and limping Goebbels (he had a clubfoot). The crowd went wild; women lifted up their children as if Jesus Christ had come. The uproar lasted quite a while until the three drove off. I later told my mother that these Nazis in brown shirts had looked rather ridiculous. This was the only time I saw Hitler face to face. After he came to power the Fuehrer did not trust crowds in Berlin and rarely showed himself. When the war began he disappeared altogether, spending all his time either in his headquarters in the woods of East Prussia or his house in the Bavarian Alps.

My father was highly regarded in the Treasury and advanced rapidly. Governments changed often and the ministers were appointed according to their party-affiliations. He was a professional civil servant and voted regularly for a center democratic party.

During the chancellorship of Heinrich Bruening, an honorable man and a member of the Catholic Center Party, tax-policy played an important part because of the precarious financial situation. The government ruled increasingly by emergency decrees to raise revenues. My father was involved in every phase of this policy. Emergency taxes (*"Notverordnungen"*), though necessary in dire circumstances, are never popular. Especially the Flight Tax (not airplane but fleeing) raised hackles. Even though with the high tax paid, great fortunes, transferred to Switzerland or the United States, survive to this day. A member of a very wealthy family who left Germany after paying an enormous tax never failed to mention this, half-jokingly, every time I met him in New York after the war. The Nazis later levied the flight-tax on Jews who had to leave Germany to survive.

My father worked closely with Chancellor Bruening until Bruening lost the confidence of Hindenburg who wanted a more conservative government. Bruening left Germany after Hitler came to power and eventually became a professor at Harvard. After the war I asked him for an affidavit to come to this country. He responded immediately, which speeded up the granting of my visa. I met him in New York and later at Harvard where he was Master of Lowell House.

In his memoirs Bruening writes very kindly about my

father who was among the very few who came to see him after his dismissal as chancellor. But he got my father's first name wrong, calling him Edward instead of Arthur. My father disliked 'Arthur' and was called Eddy by family and friends.

In 1932 my father became Secretary of State (then there was only one) at the Treasury, which meant number two after the minister. He was very happy about this promotion at only 47.

With this appointment came a huge Maybach car for official use. I only got to ride in it once when I went to a children's party at the chancellery. Franz von Papen had become Bruening's successor.

The Treasury was on Wilhelmsplatz, across the street from the Chancellery and the Palais Prince Karl (a Schinkel building.) Under the Nazis it would become Goebbel's Propaganda Ministry. I remember my father's office, a large room overlooking the Square. Ministries in those days functioned with a minimum of civil servants, compared to the present, and in this respect had not changed much since early in the century.

January 30, 1933, brought a sea change to Germany and ultimately to the rest of the world. The old and senile President von Hindenburg named Hitler chancellor after his party had become the strongest in parliament though they had lost seats in the last election in November 1932. That night my parents went to the elegant Press Ball. To celebrate Hitler's victory a torchlight-parade was to take place through the Brandenburger Tor, ending at the Chancellery where the Fuehrer, standing on a balcony, would take the salute from the adoring masses. My father thought that I should see some of this historic and tragic event and told our chauffeur to drive as closely as possible to the Brandenburger Tor.

I remember the spectacle well, the march-music, the singing, the goose-stepping and the jubilation of the crowd. Twelve years later this historical part of Berlin was reduced to rubble.

How could this have happened? Not only the lost war and the disastrous treaty of Versailles but also the worldwide depression had hit Germany especially hard. Millions were unemployed and tax-revenues went down with many wealthy people shifting their money abroad. For those not well off it was a time of hopelessness. I remember the poor on the streets of Berlin who looked undernourished and pale. The man in the brown shirt promised restoration of Germany's power and work for all once he had done away with the many parties and the parliament, which he called a "house of babble." He also would drive out the Jews whom he called bloodsuckers and responsible for the lost war and much else. Anti-Semitism has contained a strong element of envy. It is always rewarding to blame a minority.

Democracy had never really taken hold in Germany and therefore this message fell on receptive ears in all classes of people who nursed their individual grievances and resentments.

January 30, 1933, brought great changes also for us. My father resigned on April 1st with the designation "Temporary Retirement" which meant permanent. He had loved his work, though it was stressful and it was tragic for him to be involuntarily retired at a comparatively young age. Ten years earlier he had been offered a job at Salomon Oppenheim in Cologne, to this day one of the finest private banks in Germany, but had declined. Things would have worked out very differently had he accepted. He was a dedicated civil servant. My mother's brother, the head of Orenstein & Koppel after my grandfather's death, left Germany to take over the firm's branch in Johannesburg. This arrangement lasted barely three years. My mother's sisters and their families emigrated to the United States. There was no future for Jews in Germany anymore.

Outwardly life did not change. We lived in our beautiful apartment at Alsenstrasse 9 and had our butler and cook and chauffeur. Social life in Berlin went on and my parents entertained and went out. I have a letter my mother wrote to relatives in Australia in the winter of 1935 in which she describes three new evening dresses she bought for the season.

In school I did not have to work hard and got good grades in subjects I enjoyed and mediocre ones in math and natural sciences, which did not interest me.

Like all schools in Germany, the Mommsenschule encouraged the girls to enroll in the VDA (Verein fuer das Deutschum im Ausland), an association for the support of Germans living abroad. For us it meant to wear a blue kerchief around the neck and pay a small amount in membership dues. In fact it was a rather nationalistic association. Germans living in foreign lands frequently fought the last war and still yearned for the Kaiser long after he had fled to Holland.

The first and only activity I remember came on May 1, 1933, Labor Day in Europe, in the form of a huge march to the Tempelhofer Feld. There were parades and speeches. Our contingent was part of it and we thought the whole spectacle rather fun, with martial music and thousands of flags. When I came home and told my parents of this exciting day, my father was furious and said he would have never let me go to this Nazi event had he known of it. I was not to participate in anything like this again.

He did not have to worry. Shortly thereafter my headmistress asked me to her room, sat me on her lap and told me that according to instruction received, only fully Aryan girls could be members of the VDA. I do not remember that I was overly upset and no event like the first of May march ever took place again.

For minor infractions like whispering or giggling with your neighbor in class we were often called to the headmistress's room for a dressing-down. One day she told me that I had to behave especially well since I was not 100% Aryan. She was not a Nazi but I told my parents that she was a silly goose.

Almost every summer we spent several weeks in the Swiss Alps since the mountains were best for my father's asthma.

My parents liked the Engadin and we alternated between several resorts: St. Moritz, Sils Maria, Pontresina, and Celerina. The hotels were comfortable and well run. Lunch was a formal meal, lasting at least an hour, except when we went on day trips and took box lunches. Sitting quietly at table for a long time was a trial, especially since anything interesting usually took place behind me so that I had to turn around and was promptly admonished. I remember our first trip when I was four, the summer of 1926, at the Cresta Palace in Celerina. A couple with a little boy, my age, sat next to us and eventually (people were much more formal then) my parents and the boy's parents, the Altschuelers, spoke. A friendship developed that lasted for many years until 1942 when the parents were deported to Poland. A post-card my father wrote to them to their last address in Lublin came back with the notation "recipient unknown."

Every morning and afternoon we went on walks and in the evening I ate my dinner, cream of chicken soup, in my room and went to bed.

When I was older my father took me along on a mountain climbing tour with a guide. We spent the night in a Berghuette and early next morning traversed a glacier, the Diavolezza. My mother did not care for outings of this kind but I accompanied my father on many hikes. He felt best in high altitudes.

My grandmother accompanied us on these vacations. As we stayed away five or six weeks and one had to dress for dinner, we travelled with steamer trunks. One time, when we got to the Swiss border, my grandmother could not find her passport until she remembered that she had safely locked it into her trunk in the luggage car. The train had to wait until my father retrieved it.

We had five weeks off in summer but I seldom got back on the day school reopened. A letter was dispatched to Fraulein Mommsen, the headmistress, and that was that.

I will never forget the start of school-vacation, Saturday, June 30, 1934. At the Elevated Station we said good-bye to Lonny von Schleicher who lived near Potsdam outside Berlin. Her stepfather, the general, had been the last chancellor before Hitler. We had known each other for years. After wishing each other happy vacation we went our separate way. In the afternoon came the news of great upheaval. Hitler had ordered the arrest and subsequent execution of some of his old cronies whom he accused of planning a putsch. But many others, suspected of being anti-Nazi, were arrested and murdered as well. When Lonny came home she found her house surrounded by Gestapo and her mother and stepfather shot at the desk in the study.

Lonny, an only child of 14, was immediately taken in by an aunt. After vacation she came back, dressed in black. For several years she had to report to the Gestapo every month. She dealt with this terrible tragedy in an admirable way and has made an interesting life for herself. We are still very good friends.

The neighborhood where I was born and grew up was destroyed during the war. It became a sylvan landscape, so much so that when I visited Berlin with my family in 1968 I pointed out Kronprinzenufer 13 (where I was born). The children asked: "You mean that you lived under a bush?" Only now, with Berlin the capital again, this part of town is being rebuilt as the seat of the government.

In 1936, the Summer Olympics were held in Berlin. Hitler was eager to use the games as propaganda and a showcase for the Third Reich. For a few weeks, anti-Jewish signs and the violently anti-Semitic paper "The Stuermer" disappeared from the streets of Berlin. The head of the German Olympic Committee was His Excellency Lewald who had held this office for many years and who was Jewish. To replace him would not have sat well with the International Committee. Of course after the games, Lewald was permanently retired.

The Olympic Village was built more than a year before and housed the German athletes in track and field. They were soldiers who trained exclusively and were excused from

Army duties. The result was that Germany won more gold medals than other countries and for the first time professionals, not amateurs, competed in the games.

However, to Hitler's great chagrin, America's team had superlative black runners, first of them Jesse Owens, who easily won gold medals in the 100 and 200 meter races.

Hitler, who personally congratulated the winners in his box, was furious and stomped out before he had to shake Owens' hand.

On that afternoon, I was in the stadium and witnessed this utterly boorish behavior. The Nazis had a special talent in this regard.

In March 1937, I was confirmed in the Trinity Church, a classicist church, where Schleiermacher, the famous Protestant theologian, had preached in the early 1800's. Our minister, who prepared us, had a wooden leg thanks to World War I and was mostly in a sour mood. In our class were three girls and twelve boys. One day he asked the boys what they were going to be but completely disregarded the girls. That and his threat not to confirm us a week before the confirmation because we did not know enough finished him in my eyes forever.

On the night of the confirmation my parents gave a dinner for 44 at one table, the last event of such size in our house. The Lutheran pastor had been invited for the reception but when he saw a Jesuit priest, a friend of my father and a staunch anti-Nazi, he turned on his heels and walked out. I wore a black dress and high-heeled shoes for the first time which pinched all day. As was customary, I received gifts but only one stands out in my memory. A couple had their chauffeur bring in a large package. I wondered what it might be. Two huge books, coffee table size, of the Lower Church of Assisi. Just what I always wanted.

In April I graduated from the Mommsen-Schule after a rigorous state-mandated exam at the tender age of 15½. This ended my formal education.

*My father, while still
in school.*

*At eight
months old
in the
Tiergarten
with my
mother and
her brother
Walter's dog.*

*With my
parents in the
Siegesallee in
Berlin, 1925*

*"Strandkorb"
on the beach,
around 1927*

An early picture of my mother.

My father in 1932, when he became Staatssekretar.

My grandmother Rosa Orenstein.

My parents and my grandfather Benno Orenstein in 1925,
a year before he died.

Left: At the riding academy with Herr Leistner. His father taught my mother and her sisters. The academy was in the Bendlerstrasse, where the 20th July conspirators were later executed. Below left: At my boarding school, Wieblingen, 1937. Below right: Ravensbrueck, My cell was one of the windows over the stone wheel. For no reason, the unfortunate women had to roll the wheel from one end of the camp to another.

Above left: 1947, probably taken in Lugano for my visa. Above right: My mother and I on our way to America in 1938, on the Deutschland with some American. Below left: 1205 Park Avenue, 1951.

At 405 East 72nd Street with the Ledouxs, 1952.

At my wedding, February 1, 1952. We had champagne, caviar, and the best fois gras.

Chapter 3

TRAVELS BEFORE THE WAR

My parents had entered me for a year's course in domestic sciences at a boarding school in Schloss Wieblingen near Heidelberg, founded by a devout Protestant and strictly anti-Nazi headmistress, Elisabeth von Thadden. My mother thought that I should learn to cook, something she knew nothing about. I remember saying to her, "But why, I will always have a cook." "You never know," answered my mother and she was proven right.

I loved the idea of going away to school. A seamstress came to make the uniforms for warm and cold weather. I had a lot of fun in Wieblingen but I never learned to cook since I disliked the food served and thought, 'why bother?' Neither did I learn to iron. But I formed life-long friendships.

We were also taught academic subjects in which I did well, having gone to a very good school in contrast to most of the girls who came from country estates and had had sketchy schooling.

I liked most about the school the excursions and trips we took in a big blue bus through this beautiful part of southern Germany and to the Rhine and Mosel River. We were prepared with art history lessons and slides so that we knew what we were going to see. The highlight in 1937 was the trip to the World's Fair in Paris. Von Thadden was very keen on history. Her family was neighbors of Bismarck in Pommerania and his Lenbach portrait, one of many copies, hung in the entrance-hall. On our way through France we visited the battlefields of Verdun where millions of German and Allied soldiers had been killed in World War I. The war, which had lasted four years, had been fought in trenches, back and forth, in a comparatively small area. Nineteen years later the battlefields still looked grim, the trenches clearly visible. One had bayonets sticking out of the ground where a company had been buried alive in a cave-in. The bones of the fallen soldiers were collected after the war and placed in an ossuary at Fort Douaumont which we were taken to see. In the spring of 1979 I drove through the area on a super-highway. Nature had taken over and trees and bushes were lining the road, a peaceful landscape. Then I saw the sign, "Verdun."

Paris was enchanting. We saw all the sights in depth and visited the Fair with pavilions from all over the world. The German and Russian pavilions were across from each other, the German topped by a huge eagle and swastika, the Russian by a pair of muscled workers – man and woman – striding menacingly towards the German pavilion. We were not allowed to visit the Russian pavilion. The French and British colonies were also represented and their pavilions were the most colorful of all. We visited Notre Dame, the Sainte Chappelle, the Louvre, Versailles and of course the Eiffel Tower. For me this was a wonderful trip.

Our hotel was on the Avenue Victor Hugo near the Arc de Triomphe in the best neighborhood. Paris was much more elegant than Berlin. As a souvenir, I bought a bottle of Soir de Paris, then a very popular sweet-smelling perfume, and felt very worldly.

Our trip to Italy in the spring of 1938 took us to the Umbrian hill-towns and Ravenna and Venice. Again it was most enjoyable. I brought back to school a bottle of white Cinzano, which I hid in the attic of my house. Every night before dinner a friend of mine and I went up with our tooth-glasses and had a little aperitif. We finished the bottle before the school year ended.

Altogether I look back to the year in Wieblingen with great fondness. I enjoyed being away from home and even though it was an institution with strict rules it gave me the feeling of being free and almost grown-up.

While I was away at school my parents travelled to New York to see whether my father might find a job in Wall Street. He had all kinds of contacts but it was still Depression and nobody wanted to make a commitment. He was told, "Just come and we will see what we can do." But that was too vague and my father did not want to take a chance. At that time, 1937, it was impossible to take large amounts of money out of Germany. While my parents were in America and I was in Wieblingen my grandmother, who still lived with us, died of a heart attack.

Their trip to the United States had convinced my parents that I too should see the country and possibly stay for further schooling. Two of my mother's sisters lived there, one in New York, the other in Ann Arbor. So after a trip to Rome and Florence with my parents my mother and I set out in the middle of May 1938, on a beautiful Hapag boat, the "New York," from Hamburg.

Travel in first class before the war was luxurious and the food delicious. After six or seven days, on a hot and misty morning we sailed into New York harbor. All of a sudden the skyscrapers of downtown emerged, a magical sight. The boat docked on the West Side along other trans-Atlantic liners. New York in those days was one of the busiest ports in the world.

On the way to the hotel I thought the streets extremely dirty. Litter was everywhere.

At the Barbizon Plaza near Central Park South, our bedroom and bathroom were huge. Every morning breakfast appeared in boxes through a vent in the door. All this cost $7.50 a night, a fair price because money was very tight. Lunch at Childs on 5th Ave. and 46th Street, brought by Irish waitresses to the table, cost 15 cents for a big plate of eggplants. A white linen-dress, which I wore all through the war, was $5.

Everything about New York was fascinating and so different from Europe. There were elevated trains on Third and Sixth Avenues and many houses were brownstones. Rockefeller Center had been built just a few years before. We went to see the Rockettes at Radio City Music Hall and

"Little Lord Fauntleroy" with Freddie Bartholemew at the Roxy, one of the movie-palaces. On Orchard Street the pushcarts did a brisk business and the Bowery was lined with flophouses. We saw all this from a sightseeing bus.

The worst of the Depression was over but people had very little money. Apartments went begging with offers of free rent for six months.

After two weeks in New York we took a train to Ann Arbor where my aunt, Grete Blumenthal, and her family lived. My parents had visited them the previous fall and had discussed with them whether I should come over and go to high school in Ann Arbor. It was then a much smaller college-town with tree-lined streets and a relaxed life-style. I liked it but did not want to stay there. This turned out to be the right decision because I would have never seen my parents again. This would have weighed on me for the rest of my life. My uncle Franz, a professor of dermatology in Berlin, had received a Rockefeller Fellowship at the University of Michigan in 1934 but could not support his family on this salary and started to practice medicine again from which he only retired in his 80s.

After a month in the United States we returned on another Hapag boat, the "Deutschland."

Ships departed at midnight and there were lots of farewell-parties on board. We got off in Southampton as I was going to spend a month in England. After New York I loved London, a metropolis with history.

I had the good fortune to stay in Mayfair, with our friends, the Beaumonts, on Park Lane. Frank had been the British Air Attache in Prague where we had visited them two years before. His wife Cherry was the sister-in-law of

Hans Wangemann who would play a part in my life after the war.

Hans and Genia Fuerstenberg, friends of my parents in Berlin, had also invited me to stay with them. Hans was the son of the founder of the Berliner Handelsgesellschaft. Besides being a banker, he was also a great book collector. He was married to Genia, a Russian émigré, who had found her way to Berlin in the early 20s. In spite of having a house in London, he did not manage to get out of occupied France and spent the war years hidden in a village in Haut-Savoie. After the war, the Chateau de Beaumesnil in Normandy, which housed his valuable book collection, was returned to him and he again became head of the BHF-Bank. He and Genia lived into their 90s in Beaumesnil.

They had a charming 18th century house on Charles Street off Berkeley Square. It was the social season with balls and parties going on all over. At night you could hear the music through open windows just as Michael Arlen described it in his books. This would be the last big season ever. A year later war loomed and the Blitz destroyed many beautiful buildings, the house on Charles Street amongst them.

London before the war was far more glamorous than Berlin and the stores on Bond and St. James Street were elegant and full of luxury-goods. I had a lot of fun walking around and seeing the great houses and palaces. London was still the capital of an empire. The Fuerstenbergs took me to Lord's cricket grounds to watch a test match, totally incomprehensible to me. It proceeded at snail's space. I went twice to the theater, saw "Idiot's Delight" and a show with Josephine Baker, this time dressed in something more than bananas.

I spent a week with Libby Hobhouse in Somerset. She had been in my class in Wieblingen and had stayed with us in Berlin where she immediately incurred my mother's displeasure because she expected breakfast in bed. The Hobhouses lived in an 18th century house near Bath which, to my great amazement, had gaslight. Though it was July it was cold and rainy. In America it had been extremely hot. At night we had to change for dinner and shivered in our evening dresses while our hostess, Lady Hobhouse, warmed herself in front of the fireplace. There was another German girl, Gisela von der Schulenburg, staying whose mother and Libby's mother had been at finishing school together before the First World War. We walked a lot in the rain; there was not much else to do.

The family was quite eccentric. Both grandmothers were staying at the house, one politically to the left and the other one to the right. The father, Sir Percy Hobhouse was a liberal MP, attending a session at the House of Commons.

The Sudeten crisis was heating up and there was fear that Hitler might invade which made for animated conversation at the dinner table.

The left-leaning grandmother had no time for Hitler and made it a point to hold Gisela and me personally responsible for the Nazis. After listening to this for a few nights I spoke up that we were guests in their house and certainly could not be blamed for the political upheaval. That put a stop to that. The other thing that amazed me was that Libby expected me to help her muck out the stable every morning at 7:30 a.m. I reminded her that since she had expected breakfast in bed at my house, I would pass on the stable and instead go down for a nice English breakfast.

After four weeks in England, which I thoroughly enjoyed, I went home, again by ship from Southampton to Hamburg, where my parents awaited me. It had been an exciting two months.

In the fall I entered secretarial school to learn typing and shorthand.

By that time the Sudeten crisis had erupted, Hitler got his way and marched in promising that this would be his final territorial claim, and Chamberlain pronounced, "Peace in our time." To anybody who was not a Nazi it had become clear that it would only be a question of time for war to break out. My father read the London Times and followed the debates in the House of Commons with Churchill being the lonely voice warning that England was completely unprepared against the huge German rearmament and the strength of the Luftwaffe.

During the winter of 1938/39, the last in peacetime, when I was 17, I went to my first ball, the Ball of the Foreign Press at the Hotel Esplanade, an unforgettable event in view of what was to come.

This was the first winter I was allowed to go out. One night I had dinner with a friend and afterward we decided to go to the Quartier Latin, an elegant nightclub, to dance and listen to Lucienne Boyer singing "Parlez Moi D'Amour." Somebody saw me and told my mother and I got an earful about going to a nightclub at age 17. This problem was solved because with the beginning of the war a few months later most clubs closed.

In early spring of 1939 I had a wonderful treat. My aunt

Irene, my mother's brother's wife, had booked a Mediterranean cruise with her son, Alfi, to infuse him with culture before he would join his father and brother in South Africa. We were the same age and she thought it would be nice if I came along. Fortunately my parents agreed. I was to meet Irene in Munich where she had an apartment and from there we would proceed to Venice to board the "Milwaukee", a Hapag cruise-ship. For some reason I insisted on going Third Class, with wooden seats, on the train to Munich. I had never been in Third.

It turned out to be an experience. In Hanover a young man in a blue uniform without insignia entered our compartment and eventually told someone that he flew in the "Condor Legion" in Spain where the Nazis unofficially helped Franco defeating the Republicans. It was a welcome opportunity for the Luftwaffe to try out their fighter-planes, especially their dive-bombers, the Stukas. Officially the Germans denied any involvement and one could get in terrible trouble even mentioning "Condor." When we arrived in Munich the young man was promptly taken away by some civilians, obviously Gestapo. One of the passengers in our compartment had reported him.

We spent a couple of days in Venice at the Hotel Danieli. Three years before my father and I had stayed at the Lido in the Hotel Excelsior, then most elegant, and described by Thomas Mann in "Death in Venice." The Excelsior before the War was a show place where famous actors and actresses stayed. One evening a well-known movie actor and singer Jan Kiepura and his wife Martha Eggerth, he in white tie and tails, she in a long, beautiful evening dress, descended the staircase. It was like a scene from one of their movies, except this time they were not singing.

I liked the tepid water of the Mediterranean, so different from the North Sea. For lunch a delicious buffet was served on the beach. After the war the Excelsior became run down. Nobody came to the Lido anymore because the water was polluted.

My father had taken the same cruise a few years before and had been to Palestine, then a British Protectorate, Baalbek in Syria, then under French rule, and to Egypt. The currencies in those territories were tied to the Sterling. Because of Germany's shortage of foreign exchange, our cruise would take us instead to Tripolitania, later Libya, then an Italian colony. Therefore we had a chance to visit Tripoli, Bengasi, Tobruk, and all the sites that later on became the battleground for Rommel's war in the desert.

I have always loved travelling and sightseeing and this trip is still vividly with me. The "Milwaukee" was a luxury liner with marvelous food and accommodations. We always spent the night on board ship.

We sailed down the coast of Yugoslavia, stopping in Dubrovnik, then called Ragusa, and Corfu where we visited the Achilleion, the villa that had belonged to Emperor Wilhelm II. It was furnished in the overdone style of that age and became a casino after the war.

We docked at Piraeus, the port outside Athens. At the Acropolis my cousin developed ruin fatigue and at the National Museum he waited outside. For me Olympia was the high point. The stadium was then only partially excavated but you could well picture the ancient games in these tranquil surroundings. We stopped at two islands, Patmos, where the Book of the Revelations of St. John is shown in a monastery, and at Santorini where we rode on donkeys to the highest point of the island.

Our next port of call was Istanbul, then more oriental and mysterious than it is now. Sailing up the Bosporus, with the mosques and the palaces of the Ottoman rulers, was an unforgettable sight.

Tourism, as we know it now, did not exist and travelling was the privilege of the few.

At Easter we docked at the island of Rhodes, then an Italian colony. As luck would have it Goebbels was staying at the Hotel des Roses, the only good hotel at the time, with an entourage, not including his wife, but a number of young secretaries. One night there was a dance on board ship and Goebbels appeared with his party. An aide of his asked me to dance and wanted to introduce me to the minister. I passed on that.

After stops in North Africa, Libya, where I got to ride on a camel, and Sicily, we landed in Genoa and this wonderful adventure was over. I came back to Berlin just in time for Hitler's 50th birthday. It was celebrated with a big parade on the Charlottenburger Chaussee, displaying the hardware that would be used in earnest a few months later. This was Hitler's last parade ever.

Chapter 4

THE OUTBREAK OF WAR

It was obvious that, sooner rather than later, war would break out. In March Hitler had invaded Czechoslovakia but he still was not satisfied and now set his sights on Danzig and parts of Poland with a German population. These were territories that had been ceded in the treaty of Versailles. England and France had a pact with Poland guaranteeing its sovereignty, but England was in no mood for war and totally unprepared. France, better armed, was also eager to avoid conflict after the ravages of World War I on their soil. Hitler was well aware of this.

During the summer we drove to Vienna and stayed at the Hotel Sacher. Old Mrs. Sacher sat in a room by the entrance. The hotel was extremely old-fashioned and nothing had been changed, it seemed, since Emperor Franz

Joseph's time.

Vienna, after the Anschluss, was now the capital of the "Ostmark" under a German governor. It made a provincial impression. But contrary to Berlin, foodstuffs like coffee and fancy jams were still in abundance. We loaded up our car, a little Opel. Mercedes and chauffeur had been let go a few years before and my father, the most untechnical person, had learned how to drive. All went well until we came down the windy and steep Grossglocknerstrasse in the Austrian Alps. Suddenly the brakes gave out and we were in serious trouble, hurtling down the road. My mother, who sat in back, screamed. I grabbed the wheel and helped my father steer the car against a rocky wall. We were towed and after the car was repaired we made it safely back to Berlin with our goodies.

One month later, my father, my aunt Irene, and I set out again in her car that she drove at considerable speed. We went first to Salzburg for the Music Festival and heard the "Marriage of Figaro."

By now there was already a gas shortage as the army had been unofficially mobilized. Joachim Ribbentrop, the Foreign Minister, had confiscated a charming little castle Schloss Fuschl near Salzburg by having the owner arrested. A nearby service station had plenty of gas. We filled up and moved on to the Bayreuth Festspiel to hear "Parsifal," a favorite opera of my father, absolutely detested by my mother. Every year Hitler would appear at the Festival, headed by Winifred Wagner, the composer's daughter-in-law. She was an Englishwoman by birth and an admirer and intimate friend of the Fuehrer. But this year he was otherwise engaged and the only VIP present was the long-deposed King of Spain, Alfonso XIII. Like the

Salzburg Festival this would be the last festival for a long time.

"Parsifal," lasting five hours, started in the middle of the day, yet one had to be in evening dress and black tie. Dinner was served during the intermissions. I was immensely bored. One sat on wooden chairs, deliberately uncomfortable, as Wagner had conceived his operas with quasi-religious and mystical overtones. As it turned out "Parsifal," a "Weihefestspiel," was also my husband Richard's favorite opera and in time to come I got to like it.

On the way back to Berlin army formations rolled east on the Autobahn.

Negotiations between Germany and Poland were still going on with the latter desperately trying to avoid an invasion by the Germans. They were brave fighters but the mobile units of their army consisted of cavalry-regiments and they knew that they were no match for the highly motorized German forces.

Then, on Sunday August 26, like a thunderclap, there came the news over the radio that Ribbentrop and Stalin, the Nazi's Bolshevik archenemy, had signed a non-aggression-pact in Moscow. That gave Hitler a free hand in the east. Pleading atrocities by the Poles against the German population in Poland the army invaded with tanks and planes. By now Chamberlain, "the appeaser," had come to the realization that there was "no Peace in our time" and England and France declared war on Germany. However, there was nothing that they could do for Poland and in 18 days the war was over. Warsaw had been heavily bombed and Russia, which had not entered the conflict, helped itself to parts of Eastern Poland, just as it had done after World War I. The persecution of the Jews by the Germans started immediately.

Since the army had drafted all able-bodied men there was a tremendous labor-shortage in rural areas to bring in the harvest. Therefore all girls 18 years old were called up immediately to serve for six months in labor-service camps to help out on farms. I turned 18 on October 5 and immediately got a notice.

I pleaded a Jewish grandmother, thinking this connection would get me out of serving, but in this case it did not matter. A few days later I found myself on a train to Templin, Uckermark, north of Berlin. My co-draftees came from all walks of life, including Elli Uziweck, by profession a streetwalker in the north of Berlin. In camp she set up a little business by the side of the road.

There was a nice-looking girl in my compartment. In no time we found out that her mother knew my parents. Lili Merton would become a great friend of mine until she died of cancer in 1981. We decided to stick together.

Our camp, wooden barracks, had been a summer-camp for men. It was going to be our home in one of the harshest winters in memory, with arctic temperatures (the coldest - 29° Celsius) and heavy snowfalls. The barracks were not built for such weather and often during the winter we would find a pile of snow by our bed in the morning. Our Fuehrerin, a haggard unattractive woman, lorded it over us. We were six to a room and for a short while Lili and I were together. But that did not last long. We did not take things too seriously and laughed a lot.

Our first task was to bring in the potato-harvest in October and November. That was rather strenuous. We were on our knees and had to gather the potatoes in a sack fast or the horse-drawn "harrow" would be on top of you. It so happened that it rained every afternoon and you wallowed in mud. Eventually all potatoes had been harvested and it was on to beets and turnips, a vast improvement since they were picked standing up.

When the harvest was in we were sent to farms to help the farm-wife in house and garden, something for which I was singularly unsuited. I could not get over how dirty everything was. On Monday, washday, the laundry was boiled in vats. It went in dark grey and came out light grey.

One day I was told to clean out the turkey-pen with a nasty aggressive bird in it. That is where I drew the line. I told the woman politely that I could not risk being badly bitten whereupon she told me not to come back.

My next job was a vast improvement: serving beer in glasses to a lunchtime crowd in a pub on the main-square in Templin. I got five-pfennig tips and stayed clean. Unfortunately this delightful employment lasted only a few weeks. Life was quite harsh, not least because of the cold weather that set in early. Many girls got sick with bladder and kidney infections. I put on as many layers as possible, looked roly-poly but never got sick. We wore a brown uniform with a swastika brooch, called a Bruenne in "Nordic speak."

Every morning we were awakened at 5.30. It was pitch-dark and freezing.

We had to line up outside in flimsy gym-suits for exercise which was appropriately called *Fruehsport*. Every barrack was inspected for slackers who tried to weasel out. Because it was as dark as night I had found a way to move from one to another of the already inspected barracks.

But one morning I decided to attend the exercises with gloves on. The swastika flag was hoisted and saluted with outstretched arm. The "Fuehrerin" admonished me that one did not salute the flag with gloves. I told her, politely, that I did not want to get frostbitten hands like she had. She was stunned. From then on I wore gloves. My comrades were amazed.

We were well fed. Lili and I found out that it was easy, when on kitchen-detail making sandwiches, to lift a few sausages, which we promptly mailed home. On my next leave my father wanted to know how I had gotten hold of such a delicacy when food was strictly rationed. I told him and he was furious and made me promise never to do such a thing again. This was stealing, he said. I did not quite see it this way, but rather as compensation for involuntary servitude. I put on a lot of weight. When my parents came to visit me I met them on the road. They did not recognize me.

Our time was supposed to be up in April 1940 but then the announcement came that we would have to serve another six months. I had quite enough but there was no way out. Then fate struck.

In the German-Russian pact of the year before Stalin had agreed to let some of the Volga-Germans who had settled under Catherine the Great, return to Germany. They did not speak a word of German but had preserved their old customs. They trekked with wagons and horses and were housed in a near-by camp, and they brought typhoid fever. We were sent home in a hurry before the epidemic could spread. So ended this adventure. Fifty years later I heard from a fellow Arbeits-maid who visited me in New York that our Fuehrerin had been afraid of three girls – Lili and I were two of them. *Vive la petite difference.*

At the outbreak of the war we had moved to a villa in Dahlem-Lichterfelde, Gosslerstrasse 21, which my parents had bought from my aunt Grete when she and her family left Germany. This changed our life in several ways. Our couple, who had been with us since I was a small child, left and instead we had a cook, Auguste. We also had a large garden that provided us with fruit and vegetables -- a lifesaver since rationing was strict. Alsenstrasse and the neighborhood were destroyed in an air raid in 1943.

After the labor-service I had to look for a job because everybody had to work during the war. Through personal connections I was able to find a pleasant position related to the war-effort. My boss was a savvy lawyer, Erich Kussmann, who had his office in a large villa near Kurfuerstendamm. Apart from his lucrative law-practice he ran several small businesses, one of which marketed a rust-remover for military equipment, ammunition, and fortifications. The inventor of this chemical was also its salesman and travelled to all the military installations in Germany and the occupied countries. I held the fort at the office and did the correspondence. Eventually I got power of attorney. It was a pleasant job, I was not overworked and I was a good friend with the lawyer's secretary, an older woman who had helped me get the position. Nobody at the office was a Nazi. Compared to others who worked in munitions' factories, I had it made.

My boss's legal practice mainly dealt with representing rich families and individuals who had problems with the Nazis. Through a special connection to Martin Bormann, HItler's deputy and the second most powerful man in the

Nazi regime, Kussmann, charging high fees, was able to help when nobody else could. The Princes Schwarzenberg had vast land-holdings in Austria and Bohemia that had been confiscated and the bank accounts blocked when the Fuerst and head of the family had fled to Canada with considerable assets. He detested the Nazis and when the Germans marched into Austria he posted guards at the Schwarzenberg gardens by his palace in Vienna to check everybody coming in whether they had proof of being Aryan. This was in response to the Nazis who had immediately banned Jews from public parks. The Nazis had no sense of humor and Schwarzenberg had escaped to Canada before being arrested. After considerable wrangling with the authorities my boss eventually managed to have the estates returned but at the end of the war the Schwarzenbergs lost all their Bohemian holdings to the Communists.

Another equally lucrative line of my boss' legal practice was to help people proving their pure Aryan descent in order to keep land-holdings that counted as "Erbhof." It took a lot of contortions and perjuries to aryanize a parent or grandparents. The von Kameke family had estates in Pommerania, well-known for agricultural research. The problem was Mrs. von Kameke, by that time an old lady, the daughter of Geheimrat Leo Gans, the founder of I.G. Farben. Her dowry had financed the estate. Now the old lady had to swear that on her mother's side there had been considerable misbehavior, which cleaned up her act. Early in 1945 my boss, through the intervention of Hitler's deputy, succeeded in getting the certification for "Erbhof," just as the Eastern front broke and the Russians overran Pommerania. Kussmannn, no dummy, had his legal fee paid in I.G. Farben shares instead of worthless

Reichsmark.

The rust-removing business was very successful. One of our biggest jobs was to keep the Atlantic fortification, the "Westwall," spotlessly clean. The Allies, however, decided to give the Westwall a miss and on June 6, 1944, landed somewhere else, on Omaha and Utah Beach.

In 1943, the air raids on Berlin increased. The whole city, industrial sites as well as residential areas, became a target. The British attacked during the day and the Americans at night. Hardly had one gone to sleep when the sirens started and we went to the basement of our house, not much of a shelter, but definitely safer than in the city. Air raid wardens checked that nobody remained upstairs and that no light shone through the curtained windows. Were we afraid? Not really. Of course we did not want to be buried under rubble but then every bomb would bring the end of the war and the Nazis closer. Actually the air raids alone did not cause defeat but the occupation of every square inch of German territory did.

We had a wounded soldier and his wife billeted in our house. He was an ardent Nazi and one had to be extremely careful. Spies were everywhere and any remark only slightly doubting final victory could have terrible consequences.

Our cook, Auguste, had left us to move to Danzig, geographically a wrong move because eventually it was overrun by the Russians. All of a sudden we found ourselves without anybody who knew how to cook. My mother had never seen water boil and I had not paid any attention to the cooking lessons in Wieblingen. I bought a basic cookbook, fancy meals were out anyhow, and tried to teach my mother the fundamentals. We were lucky to have fruit and vegetables from the garden. Meat and fat were strictly rationed which actually made for a healthy diet. Germany was still supplied with food from the occupied countries and nobody went hungry. Real hardship only came after the war when rations became minimal and the stores had nothing to sell for worthless Reichsmarks. On the black market you could get everything for cigarettes or dollars. But that was still a few years off.

Eventually we got a Ukrainian girl, Dussja, one of many who came to Germany voluntarily because life was better than in their homeland under German occupation. She was a peasant-girl, spoke a little German which she had learned in school but she was quite unfamiliar with civilized living. She had never slept in a bed and thought toilets were for washing. Her cooking-skills did not extend beyond borscht. Every day, after I went to work, she went to my dresser and stole my underwear which I retrieved at night. It was a game.

With increasing air raids we lived now with pails of water and sand ready, not exactly state of the art in fire fighting but the fire brigades were overwhelmed. To put out a sizzling phosphor bomb, one had to dump sand on it; when doused with water it would explode in your face. One night such a bomb fell on our terrace and my father and I put it out with a lot of sand. In 1944, a firebomb burned out the attic.

Those days my parents led a quiet life and rarely went out at night. They saw friends occasionally but tried to stay away from gatherings where one might meet unfamiliar and potentially dangerous people. Denunciations flourished. It was different for young people who were not deterred by air raids.

My friend from the Labor Service, Lili Merton, gave wonderful parties. Even under the Nazis and in the middle of a World War, one can enjoy oneself when young. The men, all soldiers, were in Berlin either on leave or on assignment and would be shortly returning to the front. The motto was: "Enjoy today, who knows what tomorrow brings." At Lili's, I met Lix Oettingen, the future husband of my friend Buttel, Elisabeth Countess Lynar, and also Wilhelm Moessinger who would eventually marry one of her sisters. I walked out of Berlin with these two but more of that later.

My mother's family, her brother and sisters, had left before the war because they were Jewish. Only her mother, my grandmother, was left. My parents had, according to the Nuremberg racial laws, a so-called "mixed marriage" which protected my mother as long as my father was alive. He was also able to protect my grandmother Orenstein from harm. She had always been quite self-centered and took little notice of the war or the Nazis. She lived in an apartment in Grunewald with a large balcony and never went out. She also was the only Jewish person in Berlin who was allowed to keep her Aryan personal maid. Helene dressed and undressed her and a hairdresser came every morning to do her hair. My grandmother's only comments on the war were complaints that the coffee tasted awful and that her silken underwear came out of the wash looking gray. Wartime coffee and soap were just not the real things anymore.

She died of pneumonia at 81 in the summer of 1941. Before she could be buried her estate had to come up with RM 28,000 Reichsmark, a special "funeral tax" levied on Jews.

In the fall of 1941 the deportations began. My

grandmother's brother, Richard Landsberger, almost 80, took an overdose of sleeping pills on the eve of his call up. He had been the chief legal counsel for Orenstein & Koppel and had fought in World War I.

The first two years of the war brought major victories to the Nazis who by now occupied all of Europe except Switzerland and Sweden. Then came the attack on Russia on June 22, 1941. It was a beautiful Sunday morning when we heard through an open window the radio - announcement from Hitler's headquarters that German troops had crossed the Russian border. My father said: "This is the beginning of the end." Germany had lost the war on two fronts in 1918 and this would be no different.

Unfortunately it took another four years and many millions of casualties, civilian and military, until the Nazis were defeated. Stalin had been warned that the Germans planned an attack but he thought that Hitler would abide by the Non-Aggression Pact he had signed with Stalin 1939. The German invasion came as a surprise and whole armies were taken prisoner. Most of the soldiers starved to death. The Germans advanced far into Russia, wearing their summer uniforms, because Hitler, the great strategist, had planned for this adventure to be over in the fall with Russia begging for peace. But October came, snow started, and the Russians, in spite of heavy casualties, began to put up a resistance. We had an inkling that all did not go as planned when the government, in a nation-wide drive, called upon the population to contribute warm clothing, woolen scarves, hats, gloves etc. The merciless Russian winter had started early. It had defeated Napoleon who also invaded on June 22. History would repeat itself.

In spite of heavy losses on both sides, the Germans were

able to penetrate deep into Russia. Hitler got as far as the Crimea and the Caucasus and aimed for the oil fields of Baku, but he never reached these. In the winter of 1942/43 came the first defeat. The 6th Army occupied Stalingrad on the Volga and was engaged in heavy fighting with the Russians who encircled the city. It was hand-to-hand combat in arctic weather. In November 1942, the commanding General Paulus saw a chance to break out with at least part of the troops but Hitler forbade that. The capitulation came at the end of January 1943. There was nothing left of the 6th Army. Most of the men had been killed and the rest were taken prisoner by the Russians. Many of them died in captivity. The city was in ruins.

The Nazis had a way of camouflaging their defeats. Routs and retreats were called regroupings and the official propaganda consisted of victories and advances. Only Radio London gave one some idea that all was not well. Listening to foreign broadcasts, however, was a capital offense. At 9 o'clock at night with windows closed, curtains drawn and pillow on the telephone, in case there was a listening device, one huddled close to the radio turned very low and waited for the signal: "Hier ist London."

It was the only connection with the free world.

Chapter 5

WAR-TIME

I cannot remember that my mother was ever sick or had any complaints. Early in February 1943 she did not feel well and our doctor diagnosed flu and told her to stay in bed. She died in her sleep the next night at 59. It came as a great shock, especially to my father, who mourned her till the day he died a year later. Would she have been alive then there is no doubt that she would have been deported and killed. This she was spared.

My father wanted the urn with her ashes buried in his family's grave at the Ohlsdorf Cemetery in Hamburg but this was not permitted. Instead she was buried in the Jewish section of the cemetery. Immediately after I arrived in Hamburg in 1945 I had her urn interred together with my father's in the family gravesite, which, as of 1996, does not exist anymore.

Now it was doubly fortunate that I had not gone to

America and during the next year I tried to be good company to my father who otherwise would have been all alone.

The air raids, day and night, became more frequent and if you were caught away from home it could take hours after the all-clear signal until public transportation started to function again. One night I had been having dinner across town, too far to walk home. The air raid with heavy bombardment seemed to go on forever. Phone service was knocked out. By the time the subway was running again it was early morning. As I opened our front door there was my father, totally beside himself with fear that I had perished, welcoming me with an enormous slap in the face. I was 22 then. Though, to put it mildly, totally taken aback, I forgave him; he had thought that he would never see me again.

One evening in November 1943 we decided to meet for dinner at an old Berlin restaurant, Lutter & Wegner, not far from Unter den Linden. That night a huge air raid destroyed the old part of Berlin, including our former neighborhood Kronprinzenufer and Alsenstrasse. We spent hours in the shelter and when finally the all clear sounded we had to walk home through the burning Berlin, chaos everywhere. It took many hours winding our way through rubble and glass.

An old establishment and the best restaurant in Berlin was Horcher. You did not have to give up coupons and the cuisine was still superb. Herr Horcher had a faithful clientele and he was considerate enough to keep his old customers and Nazi bigwigs apart in separate rooms

The last time we dined there, in the winter of 1943, we had pheasant à la presse and a marvelous Burgundy. It was utterly delicious and luxurious, just like peace-time. Horcher was only able to maintain such a fine cuisine because the Nazis liked to eat there.

During the summer of 1943, I remember two visitors my father had. One was Goerdeler, the former Mayor of Leipzig who had held other high posts in the Weimar Republic. He made it his business to keep up with old friends and associates from the former regime, not without danger because Nazi spies were everywhere. He carried with him an address-book full of names, some in code, like Schwarz became Weiss, with all kinds of annotations. This would prove fatal for everyone named a year later when he was arrested after the failed attempt on Hitler's life. I remember my father saying to him when he was scribbling away furiously, "Goerdeler, put that book away. Never carry anything in writing." Goerdeler, who had ideas of becoming chancellor in a post Hitler-government, was eventually executed.

The other visitor, and this was a surprise, was Hjalmar Schacht, the former president of the Reichsbank, a financial wizard who not only had managed to stop the run-away inflation in 1923 but, being enormously ambitious, also gave Hitler the financial means to rearm Germany. Without Schacht Hitler would not have been able to start a war. By 1943 Schacht was out of power and the campaign in Russia had become a quagmire. He was a great opportunist without a moral compass and had decided to resume contact with members of the Weimar Regime whom he had shunned for more than ten years. Without calling, he turned up on our doorstep. At that time the Gestapo routinely monitored phones. Schacht was extremely tall, had a very long neck, always wore high starched collars and was easily recognized. There was an air raid and we had to go to the basement where our Nazi tenant with the head-wound recognized Schacht immediately. My father was very nervous that our unbidden guest would say something controversial. Nothing happened that afternoon but Schacht was arrested after the failed coup on Hitler in the summer of 1944 and taken to various prisons and concentration camps until the end of the war. Then the Allies arrested him again as a war criminal, tried him in Nuremberg and sentenced him to a long prison-term of which he served only part. He did not get out of jail until the early 1950's, by which time he was quite old, started a successful banking career and wrote his memoirs as a justification for his chameleon-like life.

In September 1943 my former headmistress in Wieblingen with whom we still had some contact invited my father to a tea party. The occasion was the birthday of one of her sisters but she had also asked some friends and acquaintances, all well known to my father. The school had been closed after one of the girls reported her to the Gestapo. She now worked for the Red Cross in France.

Among the guests were Hanna Solf, Otto Kiep, Schacht's son-in-law Scherpenberg and a Miss von Kurowsky. Hanna Solf, who lived in our house Alsenstrasse 9, was the widow of the widely respected former German Ambassador to Japan. She was well known in Berlin society and had what was called a "Salon."

There was one stranger at the party, a young man not yet 30, not a soldier, very unusual at that time. He had called Miss von Thadden the day before with greetings from a mutual friend in Switzerland whom he had just visited. That should have rung an alarm -- a young man in good health, not in the army, travelling to Switzerland in the middle of the war? Travel abroad had ceased completely in 1939. He was Paul Reckzeh, a doctor and the son of a professor at the University of Berlin.

I picked up my father after work. My office was nearby. The conversation was lively and centered around the ouster and arrest of Mussolini the day before, the first crack in the Axis. Could that mean that the end of the war was near? Reckzeh joined vigorously in this conversation and offered to take letters from guests at the party to Switzerland on his next trip. Since the beginning of the war all mail to foreign countries was censored and to send letters or messages by any other means constituted an offense. Obviously on that afternoon everybody had forgotten that the first rule in the fight for survival was never to speak to strangers about politics. Apparently the fact that Miss von Thadden had invited this man who came with good credentials was enough to throw caution to the wind.

On the way home my father said, "I wish I had not gone, I have a bad feeling about this man." As usual he was right. A few days later we learned through Helmuth von Moltke who worked in the Foreign Office that Reckzeh was a Gestapo agent who had deliberately infiltrated this gathering and reported what everybody said that afternoon.

When he called Elizabeth von Thadden he told her that he was anxious to meet "right thinking people who felt the way he did about the Nazis." Thadden had fallen for this, as the woman in Switzerland who had sent him was an old friend. It had been a deliberate ploy to gain access to a circle of people who were suspect but had no real power.

We were shocked. For years my father had avoided potentially dangerous situations and had kept away from strangers. The people at the party decided to lie low and refrain from further contact. We noticed that our phone was tapped; it emitted telltale clicks. Phone surveillance was not very sophisticated in those days.

Several weeks after the party Reckzeh called. He wanted to see us and find out whether he could not take any letters to Switzerland on his next trip. My father decided to let him come on a Sunday when I would be present. Of course we did not let on what we knew. Reckzeh was a colorless man with no distinctive features, ideal for a spy. After some small talk the subject of the letter came up again. My father told him that he had only one friend in Switzerland with whom he corresponded from time to time but that his letters could really pass the censor. That was where the matter rested. It was now the middle of October and we wondered when the other shoe would drop. The war in Russia was not going well and the Germans were "strategically regrouping," namely retreating. Christmas came and went and we thought that the Nazis had more important things to worry about.

We celebrated with my aunt Irene in her house in Berlin-Grunewald. She had a wonderful old East-Prussian cook who had been with her for years, was extremely faithful, and managed to produce, even with wartime restrictions, splendid meals. This was going to be our last Christmas together.

On January 12, 1944, the Gestapo arrested everybody who had been at the party. I was walking to the subway through a park nearby when several men in long leather coats stepped out of the bushes and asked me to come with them. Even before identifying themselves as Gestapo I knew who they were. The leather-coats were a telltale sign.

A car waited nearby and we drove off. My father was arrested at home. I never saw him again.

I was taken to an apartment house near Kurfuerstendamm that belonged to the Gestapo. The interrogator who had arrested me was a Kriminalrat Lange, not his real name as I learned later. I asked him to call my office that I would not be in that day. At first he said that he had just a few questions for me. But I was most anxious to find out where my father was and whether I could see him. Lange refused. Later on I learned that he was held in the same building.

The interrogation centered about what was said by whom on that afternoon. I told Lange that I had come late to pick up my father and that I had no idea what had gone on before. But he kept insisting that the conversation had been of a treasonable and defeatist nature. I completely disagreed. The questioning, though correct on Lange's part, lasted all day and all of a sudden it was evening and I was told that I was not allowed to go home. I spent the night sitting on a chair, watched by a Gestapo woman who accompanied me to the bathroom.

I kept asking about my father but did not get anywhere. The next day I was told that I was going to be taken to my house to pick up some clothes and toiletries. In the meantime, on the day of our arrest, the house had been searched for papers and correspondence and, lo and behold, they had found a picture-postcard, dated 1930 or 1931, from Josef Wirth, a chancellor in the Weimar Republic who had settled in Switzerland when the Nazis came to power. This ancient postcard was considered incriminating evidence from a plotter and enemy of the state. I pointed out that my father had had no contact with Wirth during the last 12 years. They did not find anything else but stole the letter Hitler wrote him when he resigned, thanking him for valuable service.

I did not ask to notify my Aunt Irene because I did not want to drag her into this mess but she must have learned very soon what had happened.

I still have a pocket-diary of that year in which I made notes for every day of my imprisonment. From the house near Kurfuersten Damm several of the women at the party and I were taken to the concentration camp Sachsenhausen near Berlin. We were put up in wooden barracks, each watched by two Gestapo women who never let us out of sight day or night and accompanied us to the bathroom. We were moved out of the city because of the air raids but Sachsenhausen was not much safer. Allied bombers attacked daily ammunition factories in nearby Oranienburg. The flimsily-built barracks shook like match boxes. This frightened the Gestapo women no end and they insisted to take me to a shelter. I refused, knowing that as "Special Prisoners" we would not be forcibly restrained. At this point the investigation was more like a fishing expedition. Also it gave me pleasure to see these women frightened out of their wits.

During the day I was often taken to Berlin for interrogation, which went around and around the same subject. Lange wanted to know what the "treasonous" conversations at the tea had been about. I insisted that they were purely social and had nothing whatsoever to do with treason or defeatism.

On January 19, Lange came to see me in Sachsenhausen, visibly upset. He told me that on the day before my father had committed suicide by jumping out of a window during a break in the interrogation. He had died in the ambulance on the way to the hospital. I lost control and exploded that he, Lange, had murdered my father and that one day this would be avenged, whether the war lasted one year or ten. I was convinced that I would survive but he would not.

Every single word meant a death-sentence but he tried to calm me. Obviously my father's suicide did not fit into his scheme of things this early in the investigations. All through my imprisonment I had a feeling that Lange had a bad conscience about what had happened - as much as he had a conscience. It was later said that he was one of the worst torturers.

I have often thought about my father's desperate decision. He was not athletic or a physically agile man. How had he managed to elude his guards? The day before was my mother's birthday and I was told that he had become even more depressed. But above all, he knew, and rightly so, that he would never get out alive and that he would be tortured before he was killed. This is exactly what happened to the other men. Lange never again mentioned my furious outburst.

The air raids on Oranienburg got worse, hitting the town but not the camp. On February 5, we were transported to Ravensbrueck, the largest women's concentration camp, where, we were told, we would be safe from air raids.

It was a clear cold winter day with a lot of snow on the ground. We travelled by train and, though the distance was quite short, the trip still took hours. Our guards were in civilian clothes. We sat in a 3rd class compartment and our fellow travelers had no idea where we came from and where we were going.

From the station in Fuerstenberg we were driven to the camp and housed in a prison which had been built as a stockade for SS men who had violated discipline. It was a cellblock built of cement and from now on we were going to be in solitary confinement. There were two floors, the cells down below ware dark and dank, the ones on the upper floor, where I was put, were somewhat brighter. Out of the tiny window under the ceiling I could see the smokestack of the crematorium, emitting black clouds day and night. The inmates were treated inhumanely and suffered greatly. During the night and early morning the many thousands of prisoners in rags had to assemble in the yard in ice and snow for roll call that lasted hours. If it did not add up they started all over again. Many of the women died from the cold and malnourishment and the abuse suffered at the hands of sadistic guards.

It was a shock when my cell-door closed and was locked from the outside, leaving me with an open toilet, a sink, a bed, a chair, and a table.

The food arrived through a vent in the door, dispensed by Jehovah's Witnesses who were not allowed to talk to prisoners. These unfortunate people had been in prison since 1933 and those who found themselves in Russian territory at the end of the war were promptly rearrested. The food, mostly thin soup, was miserable but edible. You could only look out of the window under the ceiling if you climbed on the bed, which was strictly forbidden. We were not supposed to see what was going on inside the camp.

It was very cold and I often wore my coat indoors. It was

an ocelot fur coat that I had on when I was arrested. I soon established a routine, not easy if you have nothing to do all day long, are not allowed to lie on the bed, and could only sit on the hard chair. We were awakened very early and had to get out of bed immediately. The Gestapo watched through the peephole day and night. You could hear their hob-nailed boots from far away and whenever I looked out of the window I had plenty of time to get down.

Every day I walked for 1½ hours back and forth in my cell. Then I played Solitaire, in solitary. Later on Aunt Irene was allowed to visit me and brought books. I reread Bismarck's Memoirs, which took quite a while.

Irene came as often as possible, once a month, a train-trip that took many hours at that time. Every time she had to get permission from Obersturmbannfuehrer Huppenkothen at the Gestapo headquarters on Prinz Albrecht-Strasse, a former Hohenzollern palace, then a dreaded prison. Huppenkothen was very unpleasant and never failed to remind Irene that he could also arrest her. She was not deterred and I have never forgotten her courage. After the war Irene heard from Mrs. Huppenkothen, asking her to write a letter attesting to the fact that her husband, by that time in prison, had always been so nice to her whenever she sought permission to see me. Needless to say, my aunt did not reply.

Once a day we were allowed a half-hour in the exercise-yard. For the first few weeks I was alone. Then a lady appeared who walked around in the other direction so that we would not talk. There was always a guard watching. I was curious to know who she was and eventually we managed to exchange a few words. She was Marie-Luise "Puppi" Sarre who had been arrested in September of 1943 with a friend, a lawyer, Langbehn, who on behalf of Himmler, head of the SS, had traveled to Switzerland with her to sound out American officials about a possible armistice. Another high official of the SS, Mueller, got wind of this venture and had Langbehn and Puppi arrested. Himmler dropped him promptly and Langbehn was eventually tried and executed. Though it was strictly forbidden, Puppi and I managed to talk and became very good friends. She was never tried but stayed in jail until the end of the war. Our friendship lasted until she died a few years ago.

In my pocket-diary there is a notation that on Whit Sunday, May 27, I went for a walk with Puppi in the woods to a nearby ruin of a medieval monastery, Kloster Himmelpfort. I had suggested this outing to two guards, former police sergeants, while Lange visited his family in occupied Poland. It was beautiful weather and the woods were full of our compatriots enjoying the day. Little did they know that we were prisoners in the camp and the two men in civilian clothes were our guards. When Lange came back he heard about this outing. The guards were severely punished and there were no more walks outside the camp.

I read in Helmut von Moltke's diaries, which were published after the war, that on the same day he was also out with his guards in the same woods. But we did not meet.

I will never forget June 7, 1944. I had a toothache and was taken to the camp-dentist. One of the young Polish inmates, a nurse, whispered in my ear that on the day before the Allies had landed in France. I was very happy.

Once in a while Lange came to see me in my cell and asked

the same questions over and over again. Who had said what at the tea, who were my father's friends and acquaintances, who came to see us, what was discussed? I had always refused to accept Lange's interpretation of treasonable utterings and kept telling him that whatever was said on that afternoon was perfectly harmless. But that was not what he wanted to hear.

The men arrested in our case fared much worse. They were often taken at night to Droegen, the Gestapo headquarters nearby, interrogated and tortured to extract incriminating evidence.

On June 9, Lange came to tell me that proceedings before the *Volksgericht* (People's Court) were being prepared and that the trial would come up shortly.

The next day we were told to pack some things and were taken by train to Kottbus, southeast of Berlin. From there we were going to be taken to Berlin for the trial. Lange told me that I would be charged with attempted high treason. Leaving my cell he said to me: "Hold your head up" (*"Kopf hoch"*). I replied, "Easier said than done."

The trains were overcrowded. We squeezed into a 3rd class carriage but could not tell our fellow-passengers where we came from and where we were headed.

In Kottbus, they housed us in a prison dating from the last century. The cells were dark and damp, even in the middle of summer. Nobody told us why we were in Kottbus and why we had not stayed in Ravensbrueck. Three weeks later, on June 30, we set out again, this time to Berlin. Our destination was an old police-jail in Moabit, not far from where I was born and where we had lived. We walked from the station. Part of it had been my daily way to school.

The jail was overcrowded and for the first time several of the women shared a cell. In the afternoon we were given the indictments, which we were allowed to read before they were taken back. The trial would start the next morning, Saturday July 1, at the Volksgericht, Bellevuestrasse. I knew that Irene had hired a lawyer, Dr. Kurt Peschke, but I had not heard from him.

We were brought to court early in the morning on a beautiful summer day. Bellevuestrasse was at the foot of Siegesallee where I had often been taken for walks through the Tiergarten. Across from the court, a former boys' school, was the apartment of my mostly-absent co-student in pre-school days.

The trial did not start for hours and I was put in a dark room in the basement. I hollered a few times for the guards to take me to the bathroom, which they grudgingly did.

After a long time we were handcuffed in pairs and led into the courtroom. It was crowded with spectators, party members in uniform and officers. The jurors were uniformed party-people. Before the trial started my lawyer, Peschke, introduced himself with the following words, "You know that I can't do anything for you." Then he retired to a chair in the corner, never opened his mouth, and charged 800 Reichsmark.

The court entered in red robes. Roland Freisler, the President, was known for terrible temper tantrums and screaming fits. While in a Russian prisoner-of-war-camp in World War I he had become an ardent Communist when the revolution broke out. This did not prevent him, on his return to Germany, from becoming an ardent Nazi. His ambition had been to become Minister of Justice but Hitler did not trust him fully and made him President of the People's Court. He was known as "the Hanging Judge."

The defendants sat in a row. I was the last in line as the youngest and least important. First were Fraulein von Thadden and Otto Kiep who were accused of High Treason. Each had to recite their life-story, but Freisler never wanted to hear the good points. Kiep had been a highly decorated officer in World War I and held important posts in the diplomatic service. That set Freisler off with a screaming fit, which was supposed to make the defendant lose his composure.

When it came to the tea party Thadden's and Kiep's defense-counsels, both very respected lawyers, asked to be heard to no avail. The whole procedure was a charade and had nothing to do with a legal trial. Freisler had already determined the sentences and just went through the motion. Reckzeh, the Gestapo spy, sat behind me and was treated with great deference by the court.

The women were less yelled at than the men. Finally, after several hours, it was my turn. Since my life-story at this point was pretty short Freisler came right to the point of my indictment, "Attempted high treason, not reporting a crime," meaning why had I not informed the Gestapo of what my father had said at the party. I replied: "I knew that Dr. Reckzeh, sitting behind me (and I turned and pointed at him), had already reported everything to the Gestapo. Therefore I did not have to do it." Freisler was obviously stunned, one eyebrow shot up and he said: "This is an argument that one cannot dismiss out of hand." Then the court retired for "deliberation". Reckzeh trotted along. It was a farce. When the court returned, death-sentences were pronounced for Thadden and Kiep, despite forceful pleas by the defense-counsels. Schacht's son-in-law got a few years at hard labor. He was lucky because the war ended on the following May 8. The case of Hanna Solf was separated but she remained in jail with her daughter until the end of the war and was never tried again. The Japanese Ambassador intervened on her behalf and possibly saved her from a death sentence but could not get her out of prison. Fraulein von Kurowsky, thoroughly confused by the goings-on, and I were acquitted for lack of evidence. In my case, my answer had obviously played a part. I did not see my lawyer again.

We were taken back to the Moabit prison and from there to an even more overcrowded jail on Oranienburger Strasse. Many of the prisoners had head-lice and I complained that I should have been released after having been acquitted or, short of that, returned to Ravensbrueck. There was nobody in authority but after a few days I was indeed taken back to Ravensbrueck. I told Puppi a little of what had happened but I had no idea what they were going to do with me. On Thursday, July 6, I was told to pack. Irene waited for me in Droegen where interrogations and visits took place. I had to sign a statement that I would not tell anybody of my imprisonment and trial if I did not want to be re-arrested and retried. We boarded a train, the first time since January 12, without guards. My good luck was that I was released two weeks before July 20, the failed attempt on Hitler's life. If I had been in jail then I would have never been let go, whether I had something to do with it or not.

After my release from jail, Irene told me that from now on I should stay with her in Grunewald. An excellent dinner awaited us.

Reckzeh, as a Gestapo spy, is said to have been responsible for having denounced 75 to 100 people. At war's end, he was arrested by the Russians and sentenced to prison for 15 years. He was let go after five and turned up in West Berlin in the early 1950s where he was arrested for aiding and abetting murder in connection with the Thadden/Kiep trial. At that time I was called by the German Consulate in New York to give evidence against him. For unknown reasons he was released before the start of the trial and promptly fled to communist East Germany where he settled and worked as a doctor. After the fall of the Wall, I saw that he lived in remarkable comfort and luxury for that country. Immediately after Reunification I tried, with the help of my friend and lawyer Alice Haidinger (Pums Ree) to start legal proceedings in the court in Berlin against Reckzeh who had fled before his trial in the 50s. The statute of limitation had not run out and he was still liable for prosecution. We fought valiantly for three years in two courts until we were notified that Reckzeh would not be prosecuted "since at the trial before the People's Court defendants were represented by counsel and therefore it had been a legal trial." Having twice been the victim of miscarriage of justice, once under Hitler, this time in the Federal Republic, I wrote to the then-President of Germany, Richard von Weizsaecker, to let him know of my outrage. He asked for the files of the Berlin courts, studied them carefully, and wrote me a very fine letter that he fully sympathized with me but could obviously not intervene in the judicial proceedings, which I knew. Reckzeh moved to Hamburg and lived out his life as a pensioner until he died at 84 in 1999. In 1994 on the 50th anniversary of the 20th of July attempt on Hitler's life, I was asked to speak at the prison in Ravensbrueck about our case.

Freisler was killed at his desk in court by a bomb on February 3, 1945. It is said that amongst the files he was working on was our case, which he wanted to reopen. Thadden and Kiep were beheaded in early September after pleas for clemency were turned down by Hitler.

After the war I read that Freisler's widow applied for a pension arguing that her husband, had he lived, would have embarked on a new career in the Federal Republic. The Chief Prosecutor of the People's Court, who was present at our trial, indeed drew a considerable pension.

Chapter 6

THE WAR ENDS

I returned to my office where my boss had been decent enough to keep my job for me. Everybody behaved just as before. But I was told to take a little vacation after what had happened. On the fateful day of July 20 I was far from Berlin, in Seefeld in the Austrian Alps. Coming back from a hike in the late afternoon I heard that Hitler had survived an attack on his life and would shortly speak on the radio. Immediately a wave of arrests started of people and their families suspected in the failed attempt. Thousands would be executed.

It was wonderful to stay with Irene instead of being alone in my house. She felt responsible for me. I also ate much better and had my laundry taken care off, such as it was. The war had now gone on for five years.

Like everything else clothes were rationed. All I owned was pre-war and consequently very worn. Shoes were a real problem. With all the walking my feet had grown a full size. It is still amazing to me how one got through so many years (it was even worse after the war) without ever buying anything new, and this at an age when clothes were important.

The winter 1944/45, the last one of the war, was unusually cold and snowy. The air raids day and night got worse and after Christmas Irene decided to go to Munich to stay with one of her sisters. Her apartment in Munich had been bombed. In February she wrote to ask me to come down for a visit. The Russians by that time had overrun East Prussia and Pommerania and were heading for Berlin. The office gave me leave. Train service was extremely erratic since troop and munitions transports always had priority. It so happened that, while we were en route, the air raids that destroyed Dresden were in full force. We were not that close but all rail-traffic stopped and we sat on the tracks for two days. I finally made it to Munich but did not stay long. The house was crowded with Irene's family and I did not feel comfortable. So I went back to Berlin and my job and the care of Irene's cook.

It was now only a question of time until the Nazis had to give up.

The Allies approached from the West and the Russians from the East. Tens of thousands of refugees from East Prussia, Silesia, and Pommerania were on the road, by rail, with horse and wagon or on foot. Yet the Nazis still talked of Final Victory.

Guns and ammunition were in short supply. A kind of Home Guard, the Volkssturm, was formed with old men and young boys who were supposed to fight the Russians with practically no weapons. The last act of

"Goetterdaemmerung" for Germany had started.

By chance I heard a radio-speech by Goebbels in which he urged people not to have much money in their house but to leave everything in the bank. That inspired me to do exactly the opposite and I immediately started to assemble a cache of basically worthless Reichsmark from two bank accounts I had. I always withdrew small amounts in order not to attract suspicion but by April I had squirreled away a filthy pile of 7,500 Marks. This turned out to be an excellent idea. Those in Berlin who followed Goebbels' advice were left with no cash because the Russians immediately closed the banks. I was able to buy cigarettes and food with these funds on the black market and when I left Germany two years later I gave a friend my last 2,000 Marks, worthless outside Germany, and she made good use of it until the DMark was established.

The military situation became more desperate and because of a shortage of gasoline the Air Force flew fewer missions and the Allies had a free hand in the air. More women were called up for work in factories. In March I received a notice in the mail to present myself at a munitions-factory in the north of Berlin on such and such a date but I threw it in the wastepaper-basket, figuring that in an increasingly chaotic situation nobody could prove that I had received the letter. I had my good office-job but there was little war-materiel left to rid of rust.

In April, when the Russians got closer to Berlin, Wilhelm Moessinger, whom I had met at Lili Merton's, asked me whether he and Buttel's sister Meggi, a war-widow, could stay with me. Irene was in Munich and they moved in. Times were unusual and one tried to help one's friends, never knowing when one might be in a similar situation. I knew that eventually I had to get out of Berlin and had a backpack ready with clothes, some jewelry and my hoard of 7500 Mark. But since we did not know when we were going to leave Meggi suggested to go up to her mother's estate near the Oder and get a load of potatoes and peas. We knew that the Russians were nearby but that did not deter us and we set out in the early morning of April 20th (Hitler's 56th and last birthday) from Grunewald station. After changing trains many times we arrived in Goerlsdorf in the afternoon.

We could hear the battle-noise. At Goerlsdorf, the estate had assembled a "Trek" to flee West, away from the Russians, with the horses of the Stud Farm and the employees of the estate, the largest in North Germany. Meggi's mother wanted her to join the family.

That night we had a memorable dinner. There were about 20 people, relatives and friends, at the table. The old butler served precious old wines from the cellar which otherwise would have to be left behind. We tasted many vintages. I remember especially an 1896 Burgundy. Whatever was left in the bottle was poured out. All this was happening with the sounds of steadily increasing artillery fire. It was a bizarre and macabre evening, somewhat like the end of a world.

Meggi and I decided to leave early in the morning, fortified with 100 pounds each of potatoes and peas, not exactly hand luggage. She had a terrific row with her mother who thought it was mad to return to Berlin but she was fiercely determined to get back to Wilhelm.

We were taken to the station in a horse-drawn buggy. Again we had to change trains many times, fortunately helped by soldiers with our two sacks. It was a miracle that trains were running at all since the Russians were now at the outskirts of Berlin. Only when young would one undertake an outing dragging more than 200 pounds while a huge battle raged within earshot.

Eventually we arrived at Grunewald Station. We could hear rumbling battle-noise. I got the handcart from the house and we pulled our precious load home.

Years later I learned that during the night of April 20, when Meggi and I were in Goerlsdorf, her youngest brother Alexander Lynar, then 16, buried the silver and porcelain in the woods with the help of trusted employees who for decades after never let on. He drew a very precise map of the site, which he kept through all these years. After the fall of the Wall, in June of 1995, the family dug up the treasure with the help of Alexander's map and very sophisticated equipment though the topography of the area had totally changed. There is only one other case known where the same person who buried his possessions retrieved them again after so many years.

The next day, Sunday, April 22, I decided that I had to get out. I said that I would leave by myself. The shelling and bombardment came closer and closer. At night, at the last minute, Meggi and Wilhelm decided to come along. We said good-bye to the dear old cook for whom the potatoes and peas were going to be a lifesaver for a long time. But it was a blessing that we left because the Russians eventually got into the house and raped the cook's niece who was hidden under a pile of coal. This was exactly what I had feared.

For Wilhelm it was risky to leave. In civilian clothes he would have been caught by military patrols who looked everywhere for deserters. They were hanged on the spot.

Wilhelm wore his black tank-uniform with his Iron Cross and I had the idea to put his arm in a sling. He had been seriously wounded in France in 1940 and had only one lung. We concocted a story that he had been in a military hospital and was now looking for his unit. We were stopped repeatedly. In pitch darkness we stumbled through the Grunewald. At dawn we reached the Nauener Heerstrasse, a major highway out of Berlin going west. Strangely enough there were no civilians on the road, only military personnel with horse and wagon. The war that had begun with Stukas and tanks ended on foot with horse-drawn wagons. The civilian population of Berlin had obviously decided to stay and guard their belongings. They would regret it.

We got rides from soldiers from time to time, very helpful since my backpack was heavy. As the army was leaving Berlin, the side of the road was lined with Home Guard (Volkssturm), boys not older than 15. I remember one who said: "The Fuehrer will manage, General Wenk and his army will be here soon." There was indeed a General Wenk but he did not have an army anymore and most of these boys were probably killed by the Russians.

We had decided to go to Schleswig-Holstein, via Mecklenburg, to our friend Lili Merton in Eutin who stayed with her sister in the house of her boyfriend's wife. Under normal circumstances not a very good idea for three strangers who were friends of the husband's girl friend to ask to be taken in by his wife but these were extraordinary and desperate times and we needed temporary shelter. Normally I would have gone to Hamburg to stay with the Rees, our old family friends, but the British had blocked all traffic across the Elbe.

It took several days to get to Eutin. We passed through a small town in Mecklenburg, which had been almost totally destroyed. The British had bombed a train at the station loaded with V-bombs.

One morning in late April, dirty and bedraggled, we rang the bell at Lili's house. Our hostess was not exactly overjoyed but she put us up. This was no time for embarrassment. We stood in line for ration-cards and waited for the war to end, which could not be far.

One day, in the restaurant of a hotel, I saw Himmler in a simple military coat. This man, who had been responsible for the deaths of millions of people, looked green in the face. He swallowed poison a few days later. A year ago, I was in jail. I found it amazing that I could look at him and not be afraid.

Eventually our hostess indicated to us that we should move and we went to Malente, a picturesque village nearby, where we boarded with a Frau Ledig. The war had not ended; all kinds of rumors circulated but nobody knew for sure what was going on. One day, pages of "Mein Kampf" appeared as toilet paper because Frau Ledig believed the war was over, only to disappear the next day when she found out the war had not ended after all. But on the 8th of May armistice was declared and "Mein Kampf" stayed in the toilet.

There was absolutely nothing to do and I felt I should move on. The mail was not yet working. In June I decided to hitchhike to Hamburg to see whether the Rees had survived the horrendous air raids. Trains were not running. I got a lift from a British airman with a truck full of potatoes but he got all kinds of ideas, so I told him that my good friend Air-Vice-Marshall Frank Beaumont would have him court-martialed if he did not let me out immediately. I did not make this up. Frank Beaumont was a friend of my parents and he was an Air-Vice-Marshal.

My next lift was one of those strange cars with a chimney-pipe, fueled by wood. We chugged along and eventually I got to Hamburg where I hoped to find my father's old friend with whom he had studied law in Hamburg before World War I. The friendship with the Ree family continued over the years and into the second generation between their daughter, Pums, and me and our children whenever they get together.

The Rees were very happy to see me; they had worried whether I had gotten out of Berlin. Their house on Oberstrasse was not damaged and they wanted me to come and stay with them which I happily and gratefully accepted. I went back to Malente, picked up my backpack and started a new life in Hamburg. I would not see Wilhelm and Meggi again until the Fifties.

The two years in Hamburg were very happy for me. After all that had happened I found a new home and a new family with the Rees. Pums was away and I could stay in her room. Her mother was a wonderful and inventive cook with a talent for whipping up something delicious with very little. When Pums came back I moved to the ground floor with Christinchen (Wentzel) and her mother, Ilse-Marie, who was married to Pums's half-brother, then a POW in Russia. I slept in an alcove behind a curtain in the living room. The other rooms were now rented out. After the devastating air raids, Hamburg in June 1943 had a tremendous housing-shortage. Still, to have survived the war and the Nazis was simply marvelous and we were full of optimism and hope.

Hamburg was in the British Zone of Occupation and a new infrastructure had to be built under the guidance of the British Military Government. The greatest priority was denazification in all areas of public life, especially in the field of education. Pums and some fellow-students decided to form a committee to reform the university which had been strictly governed by the Nazi party. They were full of idealism with visions of a democratic and enlightened academe.

They asked me to be their secretary. After hot debates every issue was voted on in truly democratic fashion. I also voted until they asked me whether I had been a student. Yes, I said, until I was 15. From then on I only took minutes. When fall came I thought of changing jobs since our office was not properly heated.

One day I met Christa Armstrong, then Tippelskirch, on the street. We had known each other in Berlin. She told me that she worked for the British Military Government and that they were looking for help. I immediately applied and became the secretary of Captain Bingham who was in charge of denazification of Hamburg industry.

He spoke no German and did not know anything about the subject matter. Bingham was a barrister and now a captain in the Coldstream Guards, good-looking with a blond mustache and a handkerchief up his sleeve. He had a German assistant who was fluent in English and between the two of us we decided who was a Nazi and who was not. We managed quite well and Captain Bingham, a family man in London, was able to spend considerable time with Junior Commander Arnold of the Women's Auxiliary Corps.

It was an excellent job. Every morning and afternoon the NAAFI canteen came along with tea and biscuits and at noon we got a nice lunch. Of course the building was well heated, so important in that very cold winter.

Christmas with the Ree family was wonderful. My aunts had sent me a CARE package which helped greatly. Christinchen had her eye on a can of sweet milk powder and that was my Christmas present to her. I still see her, sitting in a corner, emptying the can with a spoon. We all hungered for sweets.

In spite of the shortages we had a lot of fun. I never laughed so much at parties and get-togethers as I did then. We were young and knew that times would get better and that the worst was behind us.

When spring came I quit my job. I did not want to sit in an office all summer and I was going to devote my time to something that I had planned for a long time, namely to go to America, no easy task since technically Germany did not exist, only four zones of occupation. Emigration from the American and English zones was impossible. That only left the French Zone in South Germany and I decided to explore this.

But first I had to find out what had become of my house in Berlin. I had not heard anything since I left more than a year earlier. Travelling through the Russian zone was dangerous. If they caught you, you were put in jail for six weeks and had to peel potatoes. The Russians did not give out travel-permits. But there was a way from the American Zone in the South through the Thuringer Forest.

I went to Munich and teamed up with Ursel Cyliax's mother who wanted to see what had become of their estate in the Russian Zone. She was a spirited and courageous woman and a good travelling-companion for such an undertaking. We went by train to a town close to the border and then found a guide who for 100 Reichsmarks per person would lead us at night through the woods over to the Russian side.

We started out in a group at night and walked for hours, up and down, not knowing where we were and whether we would ever reach the other side in the Russian Zone. It was pitch dark. After a while our guide turned back and told us to keep on going, the border would not be far. Towards morning, totally exhausted, we reached the end of the woods and looked down on a peaceful valley and a village. We split up because everybody was going in a different direction. I had a bottle of Vodka along as a "gift" for Russians and took a little swig to pep me up. Ursel's mother and I walked down to the village, hoping to find a railroad-station. We were lucky and without being stopped we eventually caught trains, Ursel's mother going East, I going North.

The ramshackle train with 3rd class compartments chugged along, destination Weimar, where I wanted to spend the night. All over the train were posters "Typhoid Fever, don't drink the water in the toilet." We travelled through the Saale valley. Trees were in bloom and the landscape was idyllic. It was May 1, an important Communist holiday, and Weimar was decorated with red flags and posters, thanking the liberators, the Russian army. There were soldiers everywhere and I decided to get off the street as fast possible. Weimar was completely occupied by the military government but I found a Red Cross shelter and stayed there for the rest of the day. One slept in bunk beds with straw-mattresses and I got a lower berth. Towards morning I was woken up by a drizzle and jumped out of bed. The upper bunk had not made it to the toilet. It was 6 AM and I went straight to the station. The streets were empty, the Russians had been celebrating, and I did not meet any patrols. Eventually the train to Berlin came and I arrived at my house in the afternoon.

I had not been home for over a year, had not lived there for almost two years. During my absence, more people, refugees and bombing-victims, had moved in. I only stayed for a week; there was nothing left that could hold me.

Berlin was divided into four sectors; my house was in the American. General Clay's headquarters were not far away.

I had heard that in the Russian sector on Alexanderplatz a committee of former political prisoners was issuing identification cards. Though I had no written proof of my imprisonment (the Nazis never gave out anything in writing) I decided to get such a card which could be helpful travelling through the Russian Zone. It was easy to cross from one sector to another and I got this document.

At the house I gathered a lot of bank-statements and papers, which I would need to unfreeze my blocked bank accounts. My backpack was heavy and I dreaded the march back but this was the reason why I had come to Berlin. I would only take what I could carry.

The center city of Berlin was in ruins. What had not been bombed had been destroyed in house-to-house fighting when the Russians came in. Strangely enough the two biggest factories of war-materiel, Siemens and Borsig, functioned in some way until the very end even though they had been bombed constantly for years. I was glad to leave the city.

As it happened this was the last time I saw the house. I sold it 15 years later when the Wall went up. The developer who bought it tore it down and built two apartment houses on the property.

In 1942, as the air raids increased, we had an opportunity to send the best of our furniture, pictures, carpets, porcelain, glassware and books to a friend in the country who had offered storage. As it happened, our house, though damaged, was never bombed. At war's end everything we had evacuated was stolen at my friend's estate, along with her belongings.

Now I started the process of emigration.

Chapter 7

COMING TO AMERICA

One of the few Germans in an influential positions under the Allies was Robert Dietrich, a former Finance Minister in the Weimar Republic under whom my father had served. He headed the Council of the States of Baden and Wuerttemberg in the American Zone and I decided to ask his advice how I should go about applying for an exit-visa. The Laenderrat in Stuttgart was housed in one of the few buildings not destroyed. I managed to see Dietrich and he advised me that my best chance would be from the French Zone. But first I would have to establish residence in that zone. He was extremely nice and immediately called friends in Konstanz whether I could stay with them, whenever necessary, and thus register with the police. This was the first step and I was very grateful to Dietrich for his help.

The French Military Headquarters were in Baden-Baden
where they had taken over the whole town. The only place
to stay was the overcrowded Red Cross Shelter.

The Bureau for exit-permits was in the Villa Haniel, one of
the many Wilhelminian villas in this beautiful resort-town.
A crowd of applicants waited outside. Office-hours were
only from 10:00 to 11:30 but the officer in charge, Lieutenant
Jean d'Heur, often closed up earlier. After three days of
waiting outside I had enough. The door of the villa was
open and I walked in. I went up a grand staircase and saw
an elegant gentleman in civilian clothes sitting at his desk.
In my very poor French I apologized, introduced myself
and told him of my problem. He must have been quite
surprised but he heard me out. I mentioned that my father
had known the French ambassador in Berlin, Francois-
Poncet, very well and told him of our imprisonment and
that I wanted to leave Germany. I had not even been able
to fill out the preliminary forms, but could he please help
me? I gave him all my personal information and thus,
thanks to this grandseigneur, started the slow process of
emigration.

There was no place to eat in Baden-Baden since the French
had taken over all the restaurants. Fortunately Puppi Sarre
had given me the address of a friend who lived at the
Hotel Quisisana with a German who had defected to the
French during the war and now called himself Monsieur
Leloup. They invited me to some splendid lunches.
Leloup worked for the Military Government but was later
arrested for running the black market in Baden-Baden.

Before I returned to Hamburg I visited Irene in Munich
who stayed with her brother in Burg Schwaneck. Burg

Schwaneck eventually became a youth hostel where my two sons stayed during their trip to Europe in 1976. Thanks to the GI's the best black market was in Munich in the American Zone and I did some shopping with my worthless Mark. I bought cigarettes, butter, and coffee, all of it valuable for bartering. The problem was to get it home safely because of strict border-controls between the American and British Zones. The train stopped at the border between the two zones and all the passengers had to get out with their belongings. The GI's, chewing gum and rather bored, and the German police went through all the bundles with sticks and confiscated contraband, which the policemen undoubtedly took home. They inspected the passengers in groups and I managed to stay back with the group already inspected and thus brought my treasures safely home. It would have been a shame to have lost it after I had gone to all that trouble.

Train-travel was arduous and time-consuming. Apart from the overcrowding trains often stopped on the tracks for hours to let the military trains go by at great speed and brightly lit at night whereas we sat in dark trains. That is the difference between winning and losing a war.

I tied a string to my backpack on the rack and my belt at night so that nobody could take off with my possessions. Theft was rampant.

Hamburg was always a homecoming for me. I had moved out of Ober Strasse and now had a nice room nearby. The owner of the villa had TB and was in a hospital. The house was half occupied by Norwegians in British uniforms who had been imprisoned by the Nazis and hated Germans with a vengeance. One day a friend came through and asked me whether I could put him up for a few days. Since there was a room free I said yes. That turned out to be a terrible mistake. The Norwegians knew that I was a boarder but as soon as they saw Kunrat Hammerstein they threw us both out and confiscated the whole house.

I was terribly embarrassed because the poor owner would not be able to come back to her home. I rented a room across the street in the basement. Fraulein Kirsten, my former landlady, died soon after.

My application for an exit-visa to Switzerland wound its way slowly through the bureaucratic maze of the authorities in Baden-Baden but then all of a sudden the permit arrived in March of 1947. For the past few months I had corresponded with a friend of my father who had lived in Lugano since before the war. Hans Wangemann had been a respected lawyer in Berlin and was the legal adviser to the Hohenzollern family. Obviously my father, who had known him for many years, trusted him. When Wangemann left Germany in a hurry in 1934 after the Roehm Putsch and settled permanently in Switzerland, my parents entrusted him with jewelry and money for safekeeping. It was smuggled out by the wife of a Baltic diplomat in Berlin. Parts of this little treasure were twenty Mark gold-pieces, a present from my grandfather when I was born. All this would help me get to the States and give me a start. Wangemann wrote that he would put me up at his expense at a small hotel on Via Nassa near his apartment.

I packed up my belongings, such as they were, said good-bye to my friends in Hamburg and took a train to Konstanz from where I would cross into Switzerland. I still have the shabby grey paper with which I would travel to the US. Passports were not issued at that time.

The scene at the border crossing resembled Menotti's "The Consul" with people milling around, hoping for permits into Switzerland There were quite a few people I knew from Berlin, among them the former Ambassador of Latvia, a dear old man, who had known my parents well. He was in limbo since Latvia was occupied by the Russians but as a diplomat he had no problem going in and out of Switzerland. He accompanied me through the border-controls and treated me to a delicious lunch on the Swiss side. Altogether it was incredible to be in a country so orderly, well equipped in every way, with stores full of things we had not seen in almost nine years, but of course I did not have the money to buy anything.

The train-ride to Lugano was delightful. From the hotel, not far from the lake, I went to see Wangemann and thanked him for making my stay in Switzerland possible. His wife had died some years before and left him with a little daughter who could have been his grandchild. Wangemann, then in his late 70's, was very pompous and a tremendous name-dropper. For example he let it be known that Pope Pius XII had personally blessed his daughter. I had to humor him and keep him company part of the day because I depended on him.

But I got quite an unpleasant surprise when I asked him about my assets. The jewelry was produced but the very valuable gold-pieces were not. He explained that when his wife died the Swiss tax-authorities, as he said was usual, came into the house for appraising, found the gold-pieces in an envelope marked "Property of Arthur Zarden, Berlin" and confiscated them as alien property, no receipt produced. Since my position as a German at that time was precarious, subject to expulsion by the police, there was nothing I could do. It was theft and as I learned later I was not the only victim. Wangemann had done the same thing to many other people who had trusted him and used these funds to support his rather lavish life-style. I called him, though not to his face, the cheater of widows and orphans.

As always in times of upheaval there were many who preyed on the helpless and needy. I sold my jewelry at a pittance to a "renowned" jeweler, Ugo Sauter on the Via Nassa, recommended by Wangemann, who almost certainly got a commission.

In June, Wangemann's sister-in-law, Mrs. Beaumont and her husband, the Air Vice Marshal, came to Lugano and told me that I did not really have to stay with Wangemann inasmuch as I was paying for the hotel myself, out of the funds he had stolen. So I decided to move to Ascona where Puppi lived and where I was going to have a lot more fun. Wangemann took the news of my leaving very badly, implying ingratitude on my part which was hilarious but for a while I was afraid that he might make trouble for me.

In Ascona everything worked out beautifully. Puppi had found room and board for me with Gitti Horn who lived with her two young children in a house near the lake. She was, like all of us, short of money and happy to have a boarder. When she wanted to give her children a bath she asked me to put a franc in the hot water-heater. She was a very inventive cook who could do all kinds of things with zucchini, which were cheap and appeared regularly on the menu. Apart from having little money it was a relaxed and carefree life with much laughter and fun. Ascona was a favorite place for artists and all sorts of amusing and eccentric people who had landed there because of the war. Wine was cheap and social life uncomplicated. One felt in limbo, waiting for the next stage.

In Lugano I had bought some clothes from my jewelry-proceeds since I could not possibly wear the few ratty things I had brought out. I had always wanted a grey flannel-suit and that and a beige tweed-suit I wore for many years thereafter.

Ascona in the summer is almost tropical, hot and humid, and we tried to cool off in the tepid lake.

I also made some money typing. Both my employers were real characters. One, a South African woman, had written a book about Oradour, a village in France that had been destroyed by the Germans in 1944 in the most gruesome fashion as reprisal for partisan attacks. The men were shot and the women and children locked in the church, which was set on fire. The destroyed village was never rebuilt. It is a memorial and a new town has arisen next to it. The Germans committed the same atrocity in Lidice in Bohemia after Heydrich, Himmler's deputy, was shot.

I typed her manuscript in English but do not know whether it was ever published. My other job was with a German who had run a successful forwarding-business in Rumania. He had fled the Russians with his Rumanian girl friend who looked like Lorelei Lee in "Gentlemen Prefer Blondes" and only spoke her native language.

My employer was quite relaxed in his work-habits and never turned up before 10 AM. As the first order of the day he asked me to join him in a little cognac (*"Jetzt wollen wir uns mal die kleine Cognjacke anziehen."*) Too early, I said, and at noon he left for lunch and a siesta. In the afternoon he was otherwise engaged. But I was able to pay for some needed dental work.

In the meantime through Mausi von Holtzing, a friend of Puppi, I met her future husband Carl Deichmann and Rudi Hirschland. Both were closely associated with Rolf Roland, a partner in a small New York stockbroker-firm Model Roland & Stone. They urged me to look him up for a job. I had no idea when I would get my visa but made inquiries about booking a passage. I could have gone over for free on an UNRRA boat, the transport for displaced and politically persecuted persons, but, having a little money, I decided to travel under my own steam.

When my visa arrived, sped up by the affidavit of former chancellor Bruening, I booked a passage on the "Nieuw Amsterdam" out of Rotterdam for the end of October. The Hirschlands, who lived in the Hague, had invited me to stay with them for a few days. I decided to fly to Amsterdam from Zurich and not take a train through France and Belgium because I lacked a proper passport. It was my first flight ever.

I got a big send-off in Ascona. This had been a wonderful interlude. The Hirschlands met me in Schiphol. The first thing they told me was not to speak German in public. The Dutch had suffered much under the occupation and loathed Germans. The Hirschlands had a large apartment and a cook who prepared delicious meals.

On October 28 they took me to Rotterdam where the "Nieuw Amsterdam" was getting ready for its first crossing as a passenger-ship after the war. We got a send-off from Prince Bernhard and a military band.

I shared a cabin in 2nd class with two American women for which I had paid $175 which left me with $150 and a bank-draft on the Chase Bank for $1,000 which upon arrival I deposited with the Seamen's Bank for Savings as a nest-egg in my old age. The source of the $1,000 was Hans Fuerstenberg. My father had paid his servants' wages after Fuerstenberg had to leave Germany and Hans was honorable and remembered it. Not everyone was a crook like Wangemann.

Chapter 8

A NEW LIFE

Early in November 1947, I landed for the second time on American soil in Hoboken where the Holland-America line docked and was met by Tante Rosi, the widow of my Uncle Edgar, who took me to her apartment on 7th Avenue around the corner from Carnegie Hall. After a few days I moved to her brother's house in Fleetwood where I stayed for several months. He owned a small business, forwarding parcels to Europe, on Park Row across from City Hall and was kind enough, apart from letting me stay in his house, to hire me as a secretary for $40 a week.

I called Rolf Roland who invited me to his house in Larchmont but he did not have a job for me right away. He promised to get in touch with me when something came up. I knew that he would do his best because Carl Deichmann had helped him and his partner, Leo Model, get out of Holland after the Nazi invasion. Early in

February he offered me a position as cable clerk for $45 a week plus overtime which I accepted, not only because it was $5 more than I was currently making but also because it sounded like more fun.

I started right away at their office on Beaver Street near Wall Street. Tante Rosi's brother did not mind; he had given me the job for charitable reasons and also I was not a very good typist. Model Roland did all their business in foreign arbitrage by cable, either in Peterson or private codes. Because of the time-difference with Europe work started at 8 a.m. The phone never stopped ringing. I had to take down the cables, relay them immediately to the trader across from me if not in code. The decoding had to be done as fast and accurately as possible. It was extremely hectic and required utter attention to detail. Mistakes could be very costly and embarrassing. I often stayed until 7:00 p.m. and, through overtime, made enough money to live frugally but comfortably.

After a while I got tired of commuting which also put a damper on my social life. All the people I knew lived in Manhattan.

My weekly income was $60-$65.   Life was cheap. The subway and the Times were 5 cents and lunch at the Automat 50 cents. I bought dresses at Klein on Union Square for at most $15.

In spite of the pressure I enjoyed work. During the trading hours with Europe, cables poured in through RCA, Western Union, and Mackay. I had to be alert not to confuse buy and sell orders and 100 or 1000 shares. Rolf Roland, a master in arbitrage who did all his business in his head and never wrote anything down, executed most of the orders and was in his element, thoroughly enjoying what he was doing. He was happiest working, made a lot of money, and only retired at an old age.

When summer came I decided to move and looked in the Times for a furnished room, easily available then. One day, after work, I saw some, advertised for $14 a week, in hotels off 5th Avenue in the 40's. I remember Hotel Seymour and another one on the block, seedy fleabags with a very unsavory clientele.

I decided to look on the Upper Eastside and found an ad on Park Avenue. The old lady was genteel, the apartment nicely furnished but she told me that I could not have visitors. There was another ad, which I decided to check out. It was a private house on Park Avenue between 94th and 95th Street across from the Armory where Squadron A played Polo every Saturday night. The lady of the house was very nice and showed me a large room on the top floor with bath and a hot-plate. I liked it immediately but she wanted $75 a month, which I could not afford, the rule of thumb being monthly rent equals one week's salary. I explained my predicament and we agreed on $65, which was feasible. There was one condition. She wanted me to move in right away as the family was going to Canada for several weeks. I asked her whether she did not mind having a complete stranger living in her house all alone but she obviously trusted me. I moved in immediately with my possessions in one suitcase and stayed for almost four years until I got married. Why the Ledouxs ever rented will always be a mystery to me. They owned a beautiful house in Vermont and an estate in Cornwall-on-Hudson, which had been in Pierre Ledoux's family for generations. They gave wonderful parties and often included me. I became part of the family and our friendship has lasted to this day. A former renter of the room had been Grace Kelly.

The house had three entrances, the front door, a servant's entrance, and a door in back opening to a communal garden shared by several houses. At cookouts in summer you brought your steaks and a good time was had by all. New York was much safer then and I thought nothing of coming home late at night to a dark empty house and sleeping peacefully on the top floor.

For the second time I had found a home, this time with strangers.

My two aunts were Lili who lived in Brooklyn with Uncle Max Berliner, and Grete with Uncle Franz Blumenthal in Ann Arbor. Both uncles had been respected professors of medicine in Berlin and practiced again in this country. Aunt Lili was a very sweet and kind person. Tom, when he was little, steadfastly maintained that she was Chinese, something I could not dissuade him from. Luckily he never mentioned it in her presence. But he was on to something. When the Empress Hirohito died recently I was amazed how much she resembled my aunt. Max Liebermann had painted my grandfather and from a photo of this painting Tom and Phil insisted that he was really Emperor Hirohito, though in age 50 years apart. Why this is I do not know, since my grandmother came from an old Berlin family and my grandfather from West Prussia.

My aunt Grete had enormous *joie de vivre* and reminded me of my mother. She was very fond of me and we had great fun together. There was something childish in her, in an endearing way, and she was very popular. Both she and my mother had been born too early; they were determined not to let anything stand in the way of having a good time.

I went to see them often in Ann Arbor, once with Thomas.

In November of 1950 I had dinner with an old friend at a bistro on Second Avenue. He was Fritz Gorrisen from Hamburg. We met in the middle 1930s, when my mother gave a luncheon party. All of a sudden there were 13 at the table and I was pressed into service and seated next to Fritz. We then met again in New York and he and Ellen, his wife, became good friends. The bistro was Annette's Le Petit Veau. Run by Annette, from Brittany, it had become a hangout for a lot of people who knew each other. A friend of Fritz's came in, said hello and Fritz asked him to join us. And this is how I met Richard, your father and grandfather.

The bar at Annette's was a meeting place for regulars who came in every day. Annette's was a real institution, typical for New York at that time. The bar was a busy place and a home away from home for all kinds of folks. There were bachelors, temporary or permanent, and divorcees who came in daily, not only for martinis, the drink of preference then, but for companionship. Annette, behind the bar, dispensed advice for the lovelorn and otherwise distressed. The menu was restricted to huge T-bone steaks and lobsters, all to be had for $3.50. On New Year's Eve, the place was packed and champagne and drinks flowed freely. Annette, who had come here when she was young and poor, did very well and bought a house in Sag Harbor, filled with plastic flowers. In 1969, during a snow storm, she died of a heart attack, shoveling out her driveway. The place changed hands, was never the same again and shortly thereafter burned down.

We had a good time that night and shortly thereafter Richard called me and invited me to the "Barber of Seville" at the Metropolitan Opera. He had a subscription and loved opera and recorded the Saturday afternoon performances on wire, then on tape. Unfortunately that day I had been extremely busy at the office and I was so tired that I slept through most of the performance.

Richard forgave me. For the first time in my life I was introduced to opera of which I knew nothing. Through him I learned to enjoy music and also Wagner operas. I always had a prejudice because he was Hitler's favorite composer.

A year later we decided to get married which happened on February 1, 1952. Richard had a one-bedroom apartment at 405 East 72nd Street, which we soon exchanged for a spacious two bedroom. As we had a lively social life Richard thought that I should retire as soon as possible.

But I could not leave Roland in a lurch. He had been a wonderful and kind boss. My last Christmas bonus, $2000, was the largest paid to a secretary on Wall Street. It was not easy to find a replacement because the job required special skills. I knew a girl who needed the money and she was hired. She did not last long, did a poor job and took up with the Senior Partner who was impressed with her social background.

I thoroughly enjoyed the leisure of retirement, having worked for 13 years. We had a wonderful life, went out a lot and entertained a great deal. And for the first time I was able to partake of the many cultural attractions of the city.

A year before Richard had bought a cabin in the woods on Moosehill Road in Oxford, Connecticut. When I saw it first I was appalled. It lacked all amenities and did not have front-steps, only a rock. The wood-panelled living room had a fireplace, the only source of heating. Richard loved to work outdoors, cutting down trees and slowly pushing back the woods from our front door. The house became very cozy and eventually had all the appliances to make it comfortable - and of course a heating-system.

In 1952 and 1954 we travelled to Europe and each time stayed several months.

On April 20, 1955, Tom was born, a happy and easy baby. I knew nothing of child-care and through our doctor we got a German baby nurse who stayed with us for five weeks. She insisted on doing the cooking so that we could have friends for dinner. By the time she left I knew how to take care of Tom who fortunately was a good sleeper.

Three years later he was joined by Philip who arrived so fast at the hospital that my doctor never made it from the West Side. The seeds of a future marathon runner.

The years went by unbelievably fast. I thoroughly enjoyed being with the children. We went to the park every day, to Mother Goose Playground where all the Eastside children with their nannies congregated. Even then mothers were in a minority.

Weekends and summers were spent in the country. Richard's great joy was his second set of children whom he had later in life.

In 1971 everything changed when he was diagnosed with cancer and had to undergo three operations in seven weeks, one of them life-threatening. He lived another year and was a very good patient, never complaining and always trying not to upset family-life. Tom was in his last year at Taft and Philip in his last year at St. Bernard's.

Richard had a tremendous will to live and never acknowledged that he had cancer. But the doctors had predicted a year or so and the end came on June 17, 1972.

The boys have been my greatest joy. They are also each other's best friends.

As I have written these memories I again realize how lucky I have been in my life. My parents gave me a secure and happy childhood and I had a wonderful marriage, which unfortunately ended after 20 years. Now my family is my greatest source of happiness.